JOHN 3:16

Being A Fearless Child Of God

Andreas Starzacher

All biblical quotations are taken from the King James Version.

DEDICATION

This book is dedicated to my dear wife, Barbara, and in particular, to my beloved children. I pray that you will one day receive Jesus Christ into your heart and find peace of mind in him. I am very proud of you, not because of your countless great achievements you have produced without question, but simply because of who you are! I will always love you, no matter what.

CONTENTS

ACKNOWLEDGMENTS

I give glory to Jesus Christ, in whom I am justified freely by his grace through the redemption that is in Him. In Christ I am a new creature, and believing in Him has made me pass from death to life. Thank you, Jesus, for never letting me down, never. You have always kept your word. Let me keep mine.

1: Introduction

Having a closer look at today's world will reveal that fear is one of the most salient symptoms of its root cause—*uncertainty*. In particular, religious systems willingly exploit the phenomenon of uncertainty as a means to tightly wrap people up, in order to paralyze their inherent freedom of choice and, ultimately, to constantly keep them from moving forward in their spiritual journey toward happiness and peace. Hence, sincere followers cannot enter into a resting state of fearlessness and peace of mind that they truly long for. To the contrary, continuous feelings of uncertainty are cluttering people's pathway to spiritual enlightenment.

In addition to *causing* fear, uncertainty may even *foster* fear, as well as perpetual feelings of personal insufficiency and disqualification. Seeking and receiving guidance and advice from preachers, pastors, mentors, even talented speakers of revival camp meetings, and so on obviously does not necessarily lead to better understanding of truth, nor does it truly help the hundreds, the thousands, the millions of lost and wounded souls. But why? It is because most of those so-called men of God might simply be unconverted deceivers of weak and depressed souls. Their motives are not pure and devoted, but selfish, "having a form of godliness, but denying the power thereof." (2 Timothy 3:5) Another reason of equal value to not finding truth may be that you personally may not be willing to surrender *fully* to God, and refuse to focus on "whatsoever things are true, whatsoever things are honest, whatsoever things are just, whatsoever things are pure, whatsoever things are lovely, whatsoever things are of good report." (Philippians 4:8) Self-awareness of what you really want in life is the prerequisite to finding truth. Having found truth, peace and happiness will then naturally follow, due to *the law of certainty* that will be explained in more detail later. Jesus Christ puts it this way: "And ye shall know the truth, and the truth shall make you free." (John 8:32) Thus, the truth has the power to set you free, free from sin, free from uncertainty, free from unrest, free from discord, free from envy, and free from selfishness. However, truth primarily sets you free from having the need, or even the urge, to search for further truth. Why? Because there is no such thing as further truth. There is only one truth that exclusively has the power and authority to make you free.

> You have the opportunity to choose between bondage and true freedom.

The major characteristic in the realm of true freedom is the absence of uncertainty. This very realm of freedom has been re-opened for mankind by God's Son Jesus Christ. Jesus himself is "the way, the truth, and the life: no man cometh unto the Father, but by him." (John 14:6) This statement is indeed a statement of certainty, and will be referred to later in this book. It clearly points out that in Christ Jesus, every individual on this planet Earth has the possibility and free will to choose either bondage and potentially self-made restrictions, or true freedom—both states will not, and even cannot, co-exist.

Truth and knowledge

It is essential to distinguish between truth and knowledge semantically, as well as regarding their relationship to each other. These two words are often used synonymously as a means to express someone's level of spirituality or religiosity. This is, in fact, wrong, as both words have different meanings and applications. Truth is *one*, and once you

> Truth is the source of knowledge. Not the other way around.

have found the truth, it completes you. Therefore, you will not thirst for more truth because you have it already. Knowledge, however, is patchwork. This means that it does have the capability to grow in your life. And honestly speaking, growth in knowledge *will* follow once you have found truth. It is a natural consequence of truth that has been found, because truth has the fullness of knowledge in itself. Truth will never hold back its potentials that can be manifested in your life. And one of its manifestations is knowledge.

The question is: "Do you seriously want to grow and participate in this manifestation process of gaining knowledge?" Be honest with yourself! You need to know that truth is the source of knowledge. Hence, *true* knowledge cannot be received without knowing the truth first. The natural chronological order is first to *find* truth, and second to *receive* knowledge. Receiving knowledge is only possible *after* you have found truth. Remember, truth is the source of knowledge, and it is not possible to receive true knowledge without having found truth. Truth is the giver of knowledge. Unless you know and literally meet the giver of knowledge, how can you expect to receive true knowledge? The giver is Jesus Christ himself, of whom the Apostle Paul said: "In whom are hid all the treasures of wisdom and knowledge." (Colossians 2:3) Jesus Christ is the truth and the source of knowledge that has the power to transform your life and increase the level of true happiness and excitement to its full potential, where uncertainty is finally shading off and ultimately gets extinguished completely.

Moreover, knowledge cannot be found, rather, it wants to be received. The following analogy illustrates the relationship, the interdependency and mutual completion between truth and knowledge in a way that is easy to grasp. Let us think of truth as a vital water source and knowledge as its spouting water. Obviously, there is no water without the water source. Vice versa, a water source without water will by no means be considered a true water source. Water and its water source belong together. They are co-existing entities. If you find the water source, guess what you may receive? Surely, it is refreshing water!

The statement "you may receive" is used on purpose. You may find truth, you may know the truth, but on the other hand, you may ignore the truth, not allowing to receive it, and accordingly, true knowledge. In terms of our analogy, you have found the water source, you literally see the water spouting from it, but you do not receive it, in the sense of, you do not trust in the water source, and as a consequence, you do not drink the water. Without receiving the truth, taking it in, you will never be able to gain true knowledge. Therefore, if you want to receive true knowledge, you need to have found the truth first. This is the very key to being able to receive knowledge and, as a result, eradicate uncertainty in your personal life.

Uncertainty and its vicious cycle

Dealing with uncertainty without personally knowing the truth is a vicious cycle promoted by Satan himself. There is no escape from it possible by pure personal endeavor, no matter how sincerely the personal break-out may be pursued. It is simply not possible, *by definition.*

Fortunately, this is not the end of the story. Indeed, based on your own strength and goodwill, you are not able to move forward to the next level of your spiritual voyage toward inner peace, true happiness, and certainty. Many have tried and miserably failed, because their own strength is by no means sufficient to overcome their nature with its proclivities and manifold preferences. You need to get to the core of your negative feelings, where uncertainty is one of them. Uncertainty implicates hundreds of sensations—for example, fear, hatred, and envy—that further limit your freedom of choice. Therefore, in a state of uncertainty, you obviously cannot make decisions without bias, but feelings of uncertainty primarily control your actions and tremendously influence your daily decisions.

Ask yourself: *Do I really want to be restricted in my freedom of choice?* If necessary, please read the question over and over again, and meditate on it until you feel ready to answer it honestly and authentically, respectively. Someone does not need to be a prophet to correctly guess your answer underlining that, of course, you do not want to be limited in your degree of freedom of choice, otherwise, you would not have shown interest in this book and read it as far as this. Deep down, you can say that every one of us wants to be free and unrestricted in our life choices, no matter the aspect concerned. Those people who are not yet aware of their inner desire of personal freedom of choice are still controlled by uncertainty, hence not able to see clearly, and not ready for the next step toward self-knowledge. Not knowing means to assume, assuming always expresses some level of uncertainty, and uncertainty limits your freedom of choice, and consequently, your capabilities and full potential. Period. There is no escape from the impact of uncertainty once it has been released and manifested in our lives.

> Do not let any religion enslave you with feelings of uncertainty.

Religious systems and uncertainty

Uncertainty serves as a main ingredient for the majority of religious belief systems, which tremendously exploit the potential and impact of uncertainty on people's lives. Religion proclaims to have the answer to people's problems, and yet, many of their members are depressed and feeling powerless. Religion proclaims to provide spiritual guidance and help free of charge, and yet, these systems subtly load people's minds with burdensome ideas and, directly or indirectly, threaten them by correlating the amount of money given to their religious institutions to the probability of ending up in hell. Furthermore, they may tell their faithful members if they are not doing this or that at a certain frequency, they may end up in hell as well. But the most dangerous and wicked approach religious systems go for is to wrench away the assurance of salvation of sincere followers of truth.

Once the assurance of salvation has been communicated as something difficult to obtain and dependent on personal strength, or even church membership, the hotbed of manipulative intentions has been born—people are psychologically enslaved to particular religious belief systems.

John 3:16 vs. the consequences of uncertainty

The malicious virus of uncertainty has successfully infected Christianity, and in so doing, has spread to a huge number of followers of Jesus Christ. Its consequences are obvious: depression, oppression, unhappiness, feelings of not being at home, still seeking the truth, ingratitude, feelings of not being good enough, feelings of shame and worthlessness, and many more. These feelings are in total contrast to direct statements of the Lord Jesus Christ, and inevitably divert from the everlasting truth of the assurance of salvation.

> For God so loved the world that he gave his only begotten Son, that whosoever believeth in him should not perish, but have everlasting life.

John the Apostle and Evangelist records some of the most significant words of Jesus Christ in the context of salvation: "For God so loved the world, that he gave his only begotten Son, that whosoever believeth in him should not perish, but have everlasting life." (John 3:16) John 3:16 is powerful, clear, and everlasting truth. The message is so powerful, in fact, that it is worth dedicating an entire book to this single verse. Jesus Christ himself provides this statement in order to clarify his mission: He came for our sake, for the sake of you and me. And his mission was to "come to seek and to save that which was lost." (Luke 19:10)

God loves us and does not keep us in the dark. God lets you know what was, is, and is yet to come, the past, present, and future. The following chapter takes a closer look at what it actually is that God lets us know, and how it helps us to find the truth and receive godly knowledge, the basis of growth in general.

To be rescued from the valley of uncertainty

Uncertainty may be your unscalable wall to inner peace, joy, happiness, and true freedom that only originate from believing in, accepting, and receiving Jesus Christ. Do you want to get rid of uncertainty in your life? Do you want to sincerely face the truth at a personal level? Are you really open to receive it? If yes, then keep on reading. If no, keep on reading this book anyhow! It describes the plain yet powerful way out of the vicious cycle of uncertainty.

Let this be affirmed to you again: it is truly possible to break out of this vicious cycle you may currently be in, regardless of the circumstances that come into your mind, such as depression, pain, unhappiness, a broken heart, spiritual fatigue, and dead end, despair, and weakness in general. You are able to overcome if you are sincerely open to potentially changing your current life's perspective.

It is possible to be rescued from the valley of uncertainty and swept up to the mountain of true affirmation and assurance of salvation in Jesus Christ.

Personal intention for writing this book

May the words of this book help you to find inner peace and to accept and receive the truth by faith. Always remember that you are unconditionally loved by God. May your faith in some*thing* be replaced by faith in some*one*. Assurance of salvation is by no means a myth, but the very reality in Jesus Christ. To him be all the glory and honor, forever. Amen.

2: God Lets You Know

"Then spake Jesus again unto them, saying, I am the light of the world: he that followeth me shall not walk in darkness, but shall have the light of life." (John 8:12) These are the very words of Jesus Christ, a godly promise. He is the light of the world. Every human being has the free choice to walk either in the light or in mere darkness. Darkness is part of uncertainty. In darkness you cannot see clearly. Likewise, you cannot make open-minded decisions in a state of uncertainty. Your decisions are biased, your thinking patterns are biased, your personality is biased, and ultimately, *you* are biased and cannot truly understand yourself and the world you are living in. Uncertainty is the breeding ground for unwanted weeds in your life, such as fear, unhappiness, and depression.

Unless you know the truth, you continue to be trapped in a biased perspective of the world around you. Uncertainty is keeping you from growing and expanding your perception. Jesus said: "And ye shall know the truth, and the truth shall make you free." (John 8:32) The truth sets you free. But you need to *know* the truth first. Jesus Christ is the truth, and *he* will set you free. Walking in the light means to know the truth. Walking in the light means to be full of happiness and peace. Walking in the light means to stop worrying about the future. Walking in the light means to feel safe. Walking in the light means to rest beside the source of water. Walking in the light means to stop thirsting. However, knowledge is patchwork. But even if you have not received full knowledge yet, you are able to rest in truth, the source of knowledge. You have the possibility to drink at any time. Consequently, you will not thirst anymore in your life, as long as you stay and rest at the source of water, that is, the truth.

Truth comes first

Notice that it is not the knowledge itself, but the truth that sets you free. The focus needs to be on the truth, not primarily on the knowledge. Remember, truth comes first. Truth is the *source* of knowledge. There is no true knowledge without its source. You are in great danger when you take knowledge first, but even worse, you declare knowledge as the source of power and growth.

Let us have a look at the following illustration concerning the danger of declaring knowledge as the source: Knowledge is patchwork. There will always be further knowledge to explore and receive. Hence, whilst being on your journey to enlightenment, you are constantly in a state of continuously increasing knowledge. Hence, at any point in time, your life is in a state of uncertainty. Why? Because at any point in your life, you do *not* know what further knowledge will be received in the future.

Remember, not knowing means to assume, assuming

expresses some level of uncertainty. Knowledge is not the constant of the equation and will never be. Therefore, Jesus mentions truth as the enabler of true freedom. Freedom means the absence of uncertainty and the embracing of unconditional trust. In turn, the absence of uncertainty opens up the possibility of unbiased decisions. This is what I call the law of certainty: you are able to grow and receive knowledge, but at the same time, you are placid and confident in your life at any point in time.

Do you know the source of freedom?

God lets you know the true source of freedom. It is the truth that sets you free. It is Jesus Christ who sets you free. But why has mankind apparently lost the natural ability to find and accept true freedom? Why has mankind obviously lost true freedom and peace of mind? Why have people pretty much accepted bondage and spiritual limitations in their own lives and in their way of thinking? It is because they do not know the truth. It is that simple. Again, one of the most important sentences needs to be stated that you should keep in mind, unless you want to languish spiritually: "And ye shall know the truth, and the truth shall make you free." (John 8:32) The truth will certainly set you free once you get to know it.

> Jesus Christ is the true source of freedom that sets you free.

However, many people, especially Christians, do know the truth, at least they *assume* or *claim* to know it. They claim to know the truth, and yet their lives are still in bondage and full of limitations. Depression and all kinds of mental ill-health have already manifested in their lives. Even physical manifestations, like high blood pressure, heart problems, obesity, gluttony, and an excessive lifestyle mark the path of those so-called Christians. They often cannot cope with life's demands. Many Christians are weak, yet they are called to be the light of the world. They are sad, yet they are called to rejoice. They are worried about the future, yet they are called to not be afraid of the things to come. The list of negative manifestations seems to be endless. Can you identify yourself with this group of people? Could it be that you are merely assuming to know the truth? Assuming is not enough, but introduces uncertainty, and uncertainty limits your degree of freedom. Jesus said that the truth will set you free. Therefore, do you know the truth? Are you truly set free?

Examine yourself!

Honestly examine yourself! How is it that you might see manifestations in your life that completely contrast those that are said to *naturally* follow those people who actually have truly found and gotten to know the truth? The fruit of the Spirit is *the* promised and well-known manifestation in a Christian's life that is filled with the Spirit of God: "But the fruit of the Spirit is love, joy, peace, longsuffering, gentleness, goodness, faith, meekness, temperance." (Galatians 5:22, 23) In contrast, "the works of the flesh are manifest, which are these: adultery, fornication, uncleanness, lasciviousness, idolatry, witchcraft, hatred, variance, emulations, wrath, strife, seditions, heresies, envyings, murders, drunkenness, revellings." (Galatians 5:19-21) The fruit manifesting in your life is a simple mirror of the personal relationship between you and the truth. What fruit are you manifesting in your life?

The path of self-deception

By definition, deceptions are difficult to identify. However, the most dangerous deception tells you that you are on the right path when you actually are not. For example, you manifest the works of the flesh, but you are sure to be fully filled with God's Spirit. You may wonder why negative feelings manifest in your life, or why you do not experience true manifestations of assurance of salvation, peace of mind, love, and happiness.

The following question is seriously addressed to the honest seeker of truth: *Are you still looking for excuses why your manifestations are not what they ought to be in your life?* If your answer is yes, ask yourself what your personal reasons might be to deceive yourself. Stop walking on that path of self-deception! Wake up and examine yourself! Jesus is the truth, and "if the Son therefore shall make you free, ye shall be free indeed." (John 8:36) Accept it! Trust in it! Do not let deceptive thoughts enter your mind. Those thoughts are disruptive and constantly trying to convince you that you know the truth when, in fact, you may not. Or they make you believe that you need to grow in knowledge first before positive manifestations occur. These deceptive thoughts could not be farther from the truth.

> Mistrust results in separation between God and yourself.

Once you know the truth, you will be set free. Period! No uncertainty, no doubt, just pure belief in the truth, namely Jesus Christ. *He* will set you free. Your part is simply to accept and trust in this very truth.

The problem of mistrusting God

The truth sets you free. Free from what? Jesus makes you free from the bondage of sin. Sin itself is the root cause of every negative vibration on this earth. But what is sin? In actual fact, sin is mistrusting God, and therefore mistrusting the giver of truth. Mistrust results in the separation between God and mankind. Through sin entering this world, mankind has lost its oneness and divine nature. The devastating consequence for mankind is that it cannot truly trust in God anymore. The natural ability to trust God was lost. Mistrusting God implies your inability to find assurance that God really is what he pretends to be—that is, love. Unless you are sure about who God is, you can only make assumptions about God and his nature. These assumptions will introduce uncertainty, which is the momentum of the vicious cycle of defeat. Mistrust in God always results in uncertainty.

What is the nature of God? "God is love; and he that dwelleth in love dwelleth in God, and God in him." (1 John 4:16) Dwelling in love is inseparably interconnected with dwelling in God. If you dwell in true love it automatically means that you are dwelling in God and, even further, God will dwell in you. You will be *one* again, as it was before sin entered the world. This is a state of perfect peace, joy, and happiness.

Do you really trust God? "If ye then, being evil, know how to give good gifts unto your children, how much more shall your Father which is in heaven give good things to them that ask him?" (Matthew 7:11) There is no question about God's love for you. Put your trust in our loving and caring God!

The wages of sin and the gift of eternal life

Mankind has lost its divine nature through sin. We all are included in the loss of our divine nature. There are no exceptions. In the beginning, God created Adam and Eve perfectly. They had a divine nature. However, through sin, they lost their divine nature and were subjected to the universal law of non-divine nature. It reflects the consequences of sin: "For the wages of sin *is* death; but the gift of God *is* eternal life through Jesus Christ our Lord." (Romans 6:23)

> Eternal life is a gift of God to be received through faith in Jesus Christ alone.

Hence, mankind has two options to address the issue of sin and loss of divine nature. First, they have the option to resign, and the second is to receive. Resignation is an expression of helplessness, hopelessness, and powerlessness. Finally, it is accepting the truth of being sentenced to death due to the loss of divine nature. Remember, only a divine nature implies immortality. Notice that it is God "who only hath immortality." (1 Timothy 6:16) The second option to approach the universal law of life is to receive eternal life. Death is a *consequence* of sin. In contrast to death, eternal life is a *gift*, a gift of God. Eternal life cannot be produced by your own strength and willpower, nor is it a consequence of your good works. The term wages perfectly underlines the difference between a gift and something that is earned. Basically, you receive your wages once you have done your job. Wages will not get paid without being earned. Thus, sin is paying the wages to everyone who remains in a state of non-divine nature. This means that mankind, who have lost the divine nature, will automatically receive the wages of sin.

However, the gift of eternal life has nothing to do with wages getting paid once you have accomplished something. A gift may be received or rejected. The gift is complete in itself—nothing *needs* to be added to the gift, and nothing *can* be added to this gift of eternal life. If you mistrust God, the giver of eternal life, you cannot receive the gift. You cannot receive it because either you do not want to receive it, or you reject the offer due to mistrust felt toward the giver. To get rid of mistrust, it is essential to know the truth. The truth sets you free and allows you to reach the state of freedom that is characterized by the existence of free choice and the absence of uncertainty. In this very state you are able to step out of the dark and its manifold manifestations. Mistrust toward God will disappear and be immediately substituted by powerful trust in God.

> A gift may be received or rejected. It is not intended to be modified.

The way to receive the gift of eternal life

How can you receive the gift of eternal life? Let us look at Romans 6:23 once again. It reads: "For the wages of sin *is* death; but the gift of God *is* eternal life through Jesus Christ our Lord." The second part of this verse defines the reason why eternal life is offered to mankind. It says "through Jesus Christ our Lord." Jesus Christ himself is the guarantor of this life-giving gift. It is not because of you, nor because of what you did, do, or will do. It is because of Jesus Christ, as well as *his* work that he has accomplished here on Earth. Therefore, the angels declare with a loud voice: "Worthy is the Lamb." (Revelation 5:12)

But what has Jesus done for us? God "hath not appointed us to wrath, but to obtain salvation by our Lord Jesus Christ, who died for us, that, whether we wake or sleep, we should live together with him." (1 Thessalonians 5:9, 10). Clearly, God's plan for us is to obtain salvation by Jesus Christ, who put away sin. We must die because of sin and our non-divine nature. However, we have the choice to receive the gift of eternal life through accepting Jesus Christ and his work being sufficient for our salvation.

We need to receive Jesus. "But as many as received him, to them gave he power to become the sons of God, even to them that believe on his name: which were born, not of blood, nor of the will of the flesh, nor of the will of man, but of God." (John 1:12, 13) This verse is very powerful and explains the truth in one of the most precious and unambiguous ways: if you *receive* Christ, you become a child of God, a member of the body, that is, Jesus Christ.

A child of God is a partaker of the divine nature. (2 Peter 1:4) Once you believe in the Son of God, Jesus Christ, you are *in* Christ and hence, a new creature. "Therefore, if any man *be* in Christ, he *is* a new creature: old things are passed away; behold, all things are become new." (2 Corinthians 5:17) In Christ we are a new creation and partakers of the divine nature. A divine nature intrinsically contains immortality bestowed by God through Jesus Christ. *To believe or not to believe*—your eternal future depends on your personal response to God's gentle invitation to receive the gift of eternal life through Jesus Christ.

The short answer to the question of how to receive the gift of eternal life is: believe in Jesus Christ. You need to trust Jesus to receive eternal life.

A peek behind the curtains

God lets you know the truth. So far, we have seen sin being successfully dealt with by Jesus Christ, who died for us, so "that whosoever believeth in him should not perish, but have everlasting life." (John 3:16) Unless we accept Jesus Christ and truly believe in him, we cannot receive God's gift of eternal life. In his letter to the Ephesians, the Apostle Paul provides further insights, allowing us to peek behind the curtains and have an impressive glimpse into the spiritual realm. "For we wrestle not against flesh and blood, but against principalities, against powers, against the rulers of the darkness of this world, against spiritual wickedness in high places." (Ephesians 6:12)

Once you believe in Jesus and accept him as Lord, once you are born of God, once you become a child of God and partaker of the divine nature, you are actively participating in a spiritual war on a spiritual battlefield. The good news is that the battle has already been won by Jesus Christ. Therefore, even our personal battle can be victoriously mastered by clinging tightly to Jesus, the Son of God.

The armor of God

The enemy is not of flesh and blood. How can you protect yourself? "Wherefore take unto you the whole armor of God, that ye may be able to withstand in the evil day, and having done all, to stand." (Ephesians 6:13) Obviously, you cannot survive with conventional war weapons.

That is why God lets you know the whole armor which has the power to protect the spiritual dimension of your life. The armor should be put on to be able to withstand pressures in the evil day. Thus, you need to equip yourself in advance,

> Put on the armor of God to be prepared for the great spiritual battle in your life.

so that you are ready for the evil day. You might have a problem if you try to put on the armor on the very day the war begins. Be prepared in advance!

The armor consists of six components. "Stand therefore, having your loins girt about with truth, and having on the breastplate of righteousness; and your feet shod with the preparation of the gospel of peace; above all, taking the shield of faith, wherewith ye shall be able to quench all the fiery darts of the wicked. And take the helmet of salvation, and the sword of the Spirit, which is the word of God." (Ephesians 6:14-17)

First, *the belt of truth*. It holds everything together. Jesus Christ is the truth that sets you free, moves you to the highest spiritual level of personal freedom, and eradicates uncertainty in your life. He is the solid foundation.

Second, *the breastplate of righteousness*. The breastplate protects the heart. This is significant, as God points out to "keep thy heart with all diligence; for out of it are the issues of life." (Proverbs 4:23) An unprotected heart is like an open fortress that is easily captured and conquered. So be aware and diligently take on the breastplate of righteousness. But what is righteousness? "But of him are ye in Christ Jesus, who of God is made unto us wisdom, and righteousness, and sanctification, and redemption." (1 Corinthians 1:30) Jesus is our righteousness. Believing in Christ and accepting the gift of salvation means right standing before God. It is not your own righteousness. It is the righteousness of Christ that has the power to save you and move you toward inner peace, happiness, and certainty. Your heart is protected by the breastplate of Christ's righteousness against any accusations of the enemy. Why? Because in Christ you are already righteous. You do not need to perform anything in your life to reach the level of being righteous. If the enemy tries to convince you of how unworthy you are, all you need to do is point to Jesus and declare his perfect righteousness, which, by faith, is imputed unto you. Therefore, be certain of your right standing before God!

Third, *the gospel of peace*. Peace is the result of total trust. It originates from the source, God. Peace is brought unto you through Jesus Christ. These are his very words: "Peace I leave with you, my peace I give unto you: not as the world giveth, give I unto you. Let not your heart be troubled, neither let it be afraid." (John 14:27) It is only Jesus who gives peace from a higher spiritual level than the world is capable of doing. Worldly peace is dependent on circumstances. Jesus provides unlimited peace of mind. Accept and receive it by faith and trust! Let your heart not be troubled nor let it be afraid. Troubles, doubts, and fear tremendously decrease your energy level.

That is why Jesus himself encourages you to think positively and focus on "whatsoever things are true, whatsoever things are honest, whatsoever things are just, whatsoever things are pure, whatsoever things are lovely, whatsoever things are of good report." (Philippians 4:8)

Fourth, *the shield of faith*. It protects you from various kinds of attacks on a physical as well as an emotional level. Fiery darts of the wicked may be shot toward you in various forms of doubts. For example, worry that you are not good enough, feelings your wife or your husband is not good enough for you, that you are not valuable, and so forth. Do not meditate on doubtful statements or even doubtful thoughts, but trust in Jesus. Faith in him and his righteousness has the power to quench all the fiery darts. These darts come to nothing, because Jesus has already overcome the world. And by putting your faith in Jesus and his finished work on the cross, you will also overcome the world. Thus, make good use of the shield of faith in Jesus Christ!

Fifth, *the helmet of salvation.* Jesus is your salvation. It is his work that justifies you before God. "Who was delivered for our offences, and was raised again for our justification." (Romans 4:25) Jesus is your justification that saves you from the wages of sin. It has the power to transform your life from a non-divine nature that is subject to death, to a partaker of the divine nature that leads to oneness and eternal life. The helmet wants to protect your head, which is the center of thoughts and feelings. Any attacks toward thoughts have a decisive impact on the whole human organism. Therefore, you are invited to *take* the helmet of salvation. But listen, you are only able to take what is already available to be taken. What does that teach us? Salvation has already been accomplished. Nothing has to be done except to take it. The helmet of salvation reminds you that your salvation is not dependent on what you do, but rather, on what has already been done by Jesus Christ *for* you. Let this fact permeate your thoughts.

Sixth, *the sword of the Spirit.* The sword of the Spirit is the word of God. In contrast to the previous five components of the whole armor of God, the sword of the Spirit is an offensive weapon. The other five components are defensive in nature. The word of God "is quick, and powerful, and sharper than any two-edged sword, piercing even to the dividing asunder of soul and spirit, and of the joints and marrow, and is a discerner of the thoughts and intents of the heart." (Hebrews 4:12) God's word affects your entire being, your flesh and bones, and even your thoughts. The word of God is comparable to a constant. It does not change. "The grass withereth, the flower fadeth: but the word of our God shall stand forever." (Isaiah 40:8) You can fully trust and rely on the word of God.

The whole armor of God is provided for us to gain victory in our spiritual life. "Finally, my brethren, be strong in the Lord, and in the power of his might." (Ephesians 6:10) It is not *our* strength that brings us victory, but it is the power of Jesus Christ working in us. God provides hope and assurance "that at the name of Jesus every knee should bow, of things in heaven, and things in earth, and things under the earth." (Philippians 2:10) If we are in Christ, we will certainly be victorious warriors within the spiritual war. Be assured of being a winner in Christ.

> Healing occurs in an atmosphere of trust. You find both in the presence of Jesus Christ.

Thoughts: an atmosphere of trust and healing

God lets you know the truth about thoughts. In the context of the armor of God, the helmet of salvation was mentioned as an essential component of that armor. It plays a significant role in its function to protect the head, and even the thoughts. Thoughts have a tremendous impact on our body, as well as our spiritual well-being. Jesus knows every thought: "And Jesus, knowing their thoughts, said,

'Wherefore think ye evil in your hearts?' " (Matthew 9:4) We are an open book. Whatever we do or think, God is fully aware of it already. Knowing that God is aware of every aspect of your life may cause discomfort. But why? Maybe you make yourself feel bad about something that you do in your life, something you do not want anybody to know about. In general, discomfort is a consequence of uncertainty or mistrust.

For the sake of illustration, let us assume you want to hide your alcohol addiction and pretend to live a life without any addiction. Why do you want to hide it? What are potential reasons for your fake life? For example, you might be proud and do not want to damage your reputation. This means that you do not trust society that it will not condemn you because of what you really are. Does hiding your addiction really help you to overcome it, though? The answer is no. It does not help you at all. Instead of hiding your problem, let us now assume you attend an Alcoholics Anonymous group. You now openly talk about your addiction. Why? Because you do not fear or expect any negative response from within this group. Each participant of the group is there to respect each other. There is a common feeling of trust and respect and an attitude of wanting to help each other. In the end, every participant knows that the other group members are all in the same boat. Again the question: does such a trustful environment help you to get rid of your addiction? Most likely, the answer will be yes. Why? Because healing occurs in an atmosphere of trust. This is exactly what Jesus offers us freely.

Jesus says: "Come unto me, all ye that labour and are heavy laden, and I will give you rest." (Matthew 11:28) He wants to heal you. "Confess your faults one to another, and pray one for another, that ye may be healed. The effectual fervent prayer of a righteous man availeth much." (James 5:16) Confessing in prayer is an effective tool to receive healing. Jesus is *for*, not against you. In the presence of Jesus you feel safe, loved, and truly accepted. As a consequence, you do not need to be worried at all about him knowing your deepest thoughts. Think about it!

Thoughts: the quality gate for your thoughts

Thoughts are powerful, yet utterly vulnerable. Your thoughts need to be controlled by you or they will surely get controlled by others. Take care of your thoughts. Positive as well as negative vibrations and their manifestations originate from your thoughts. Moreover, thoughts of others may try to enter your mind and finally be manifested in your life. They will influence your thinking pattern, having a strong influence on your way of living in this world. You need to sort of filter incoming vibrations according to some quality gate. Every thought should be required to pass this gate. What is the quality gate? Once truth has been found, the quality gate is based on knowledge. As knowledge, the quality gate is constantly evolving, but it is guaranteed that it

> The way you think determines who you are. It is based on the law of sowing and harvesting.

evolves in accordance with the will of God. It is essential to make use of a proper quality gate for your thoughts. It is the way you think that determines who you *are*. Look at what God tells you right now: "For as he thinketh in his heart, so is he." (Proverbs 23:7) In the epistle to the followers of Christ in Galatia, Paul puts it this way: "For whatsoever a man soweth, that shall he also reap." (Galatians 6:7) It is the same basic message as in Proverbs 23:7. It explains the law of *sowing and harvesting*. No matter if you are sowing a physical entity, for example flower seeds, or a thought. Its manifestation is going to happen regardless of the *nature* of the seed. Thoughts have the power to transform your life. This is not mere theory, but the key to stopping negative manifestations in your life. This is the reason why God lets you know the truth about thoughts and their power. Thoughts have a strong impact on your life, but also on the lives of others.

For example, if you think badly of someone, you are sowing negative seeds toward this person. What will be the result according to the law of sowing and harvesting? You will again reap negative manifestations and restrict your degree of freedom. Here is an illustration: adultery. Jesus' message on that topic is notable: "But I say unto you, That whosoever looketh on a woman to lust after her hath committed adultery with her already in his heart." (Matthew 5:28) Jesus is saying that you commit adultery even when you look lustfully on a woman. Is this too restrictive for you? Where does looking lustfully begin? It begins with a thought in your mind.

On a spiritual level, this very thought of lustfully looking on a woman has, in fact, the same harvest as if you choose to act it out literally. In both cases the outcome is committing adultery. Jesus precisely warns people to "speak not evil one of another." (James 4:11) Because of the impact you generate toward them and your own life, respectively. Control your thoughts, and it will transform your life accordingly!

If you do not have a knowledge-based quality gate set up for your thoughts to pass through before making decisions, it is very likely you will be deceived by some inner forces within you, and also by external influences, respectively. But remember, you need to have found the truth first in order to be able to receive true knowledge. Only then is

> The originator of the lie, the devil, does not wait till you pass his lair. He is actively seeking those who he can devour.

it possible to establish a quality gate based on knowledge, ready to filter deceptive information out.

Deception and its influence on your life

Deception has a tremendous impact on your entire life. It is very difficult to escape deceptive influences once you have been captured by them. However, what exactly does the term deception mean? First, deception makes use of lies, and tries to convince you to, for example, believe, buy, or love something that is not of value. Second, it wants you to exchange something of assumed inferior value for something that is assumed to be of value, for instance, exchanging eternal life for eternal condemnation, faithful marriage for adultery, love for hate, trust for distrust, assurance for uncertainty. All examples of deception have one common denominator, namely, they systematically lead you away from God, the source of true freedom, peace of mind, and from the truth which is Jesus Christ.

Lies are the basis of deception. They are the opposite of truth. Jesus mentions the one who is the originator of the lie, and thus deception, namely the devil himself. Notice what

Jesus says about the lie and its originator when he is discussing this matter with the Pharisees: "Ye are of your father the devil, and the lusts of your father ye will do. He was a murderer from the beginning, and abode not in the truth, because there is no truth in him. When he speaketh a lie, he speaketh of his own: for he is a liar, and the father of it." (John 8:44) Jesus calls the devil the father of the lie.

There is no truth in the devil. Hence, the things he says are simply not true. The devil wants you to believe in him and his lies nonetheless. His aspirations are not clumsy or easily exposed. The exact opposite is true: he approaches mankind with his deceptions in a subtle way that cannot easily be revealed by superficial observation. Great are his efforts to achieve his goals to devour his explicit enemies, namely the true followers of Christ.

In his first letter to the followers of Jesus who were scattered throughout Pontus, Galatia, Cappadocia, Asia, and Bithynia, Peter, the Apostle of Jesus Christ, sums it up in a nutshell: "Be sober, be vigilant; because your adversary the devil, as a roaring lion, walketh about, seeking whom he may devour: whom resist steadfast in the faith." (1 Peter 5:8, 9) Peter compares the devil with a roaring lion ready to devour everything that is possible. Interestingly, the devil *is* actively *seeking*. He is not waiting till someone happens to pass his lair, but is *looking* for anyone he can devour. As a consequence, deception will actively knock at the door of your mind, or rather, try to cunningly enter through its back door. Jesus advises the true seeker of truth and knowledge to be open-minded, yet cautious and vigilant: "Take heed lest any man deceive you: For many shall come in my name, saying, 'I am Christ'; and shall deceive many." (Mark 13:5, 6)

God loves you. It is because of his love that God lets you know that deception is nothing more than a sophisticated and highly elaborate lie whose father is the devil himself. Thousands of people are victims of deception. Those people do not know the truth. If they had come to know it, they would have been set free by Jesus Christ himself. They would have never been victims of deception. Why? Because in order to be a victim of deception you need to be a victim of the devil.

Once you are a new creature in Christ your life has been transformed from a non-divine nature to a partaker of the divine nature. In the spiritual realm there has been a change in sovereignty—from death to life, from darkness to light, from Satan to Christ.

By *receiving* Christ by faith, you now no longer belong to the devil's governance. This is indeed good news! Deception is one of the most effective weapons of the devil, and it constantly whispers doubt and uncertainty into your ear. But the power of deception is gone once you have received Christ. Why is that? It is because deception and its diverse manifestations are not part of truth, but falsehood. If you are in the truth, you see clearly and are able to distinguish between truth and falsehood. Find out yourself by receiving Christ!

Receiving Christ and exposing deception

God lets you know how to expose deception. It is by receiving Christ. You shift from sin's slavery to being a child of God. But what does it actually mean to receive Christ? Let us shortly explore the verb "receive." The Greek word for it is "lambano," which has a variety of meanings, such as to *take*, to *seize*, to *admit*, and to *choose*. Basically, it means to *receive what is given*. God offers eternal life "and this life is in his Son." (1 John 5:11) If you have received God's Son, you have received the gift of eternal life.

So it is worth knowing *how* to receive Christ in your life. Jesus himself proclaims: "Verily, verily, I say unto you, He that heareth my word, and believeth on him that sent me, hath everlasting life, and shall not come into condemnation; but is passed from death unto life." (John 5:24) Hence, to receive Christ means to believe in him and accept Jesus as Lord and Savior. To receive is somehow correlated to the verb to believe. If you do not believe, it is impossible to receive. You can only receive when you believe. "But without faith it is impossible to please him: for he that cometh to God must believe that he is, and that he is a rewarder of them that diligently seek him." (Hebrews 11:6) He who believes in Jesus has everlasting life. Condemnation will not be sin's consequence for a child of God, because Jesus dealt with its consequence in that he died for us and rose again from the dead. As God's child, your eyes have been opened to see the spiritual reality. God has raised your awareness for it. Therefore, as a child of God, you are empowered to be able to expose deceptions of any kind.

Being saved by grace through faith

Remember that eternal life is a gift of God that we can receive through Jesus Christ. In addition, Paul mentions the importance of faith in the context of receiving in his letter to the Ephesians: "For by grace are ye saved through faith; and that not of yourselves: it is the gift of God: not of works, lest any man should boast." (Ephesians 2:8, 9) It says we are saved by grace through faith. The gift of God is eternal salvation. To be saved means to have already received eternal life.

But what does it mean to be saved by grace through faith? First, the context of this verse tells us that grace is offered by God and it brings salvation to the receiver. Grace is something that cannot be earned by works or any kind of endeavor. Indeed, grace is a gift and a characteristic of God. God is gracious. God is offering eternal life through his Son Jesus Christ. Because of God's grace and love, he sent his Son to Earth, to redeem us from the bondage of sin and restricted freedom of choice due to any excesses of uncertainty. Grace is offered by God, and it can be accepted and received *through faith* or rejected. The emphasis is on "through faith."

Second, it is *faith* that enables you to receive what God has already provided for you. God defines the term faith in the book of Hebrews as follows: "Now faith is the substance of things hoped for, the evidence of things not seen." (Hebrews 11:1) So what are you waiting for? Thankfully make use of God's grace and receive it through faith!

> Eternal salvation is a gift from God to everyone who receives Christ. And faith is the basis to receive.

Faith is having trust in God

Faith is *the* substance and the basis to personally receive Jesus Christ, and to be partakers of eternal life in him. Faith is not a mere human achievement, but "cometh by hearing, and hearing by the word of God." (Romans 10:17) Faith is a result of hearing the word of God. Thus, the originator of faith is God himself.

Furthermore, faith is having trust in God. If you trust God with your heart then you will believe in him, and whatever he is saying you will willingly accept with pleasure. God is good "who will have all men to be saved, and to come unto the knowledge of the truth." (1 Timothy 2:4) Yet again, it is the knowledge of truth you need to receive in your life, especially in your mind. Once you get to know the truth, you will see the goodness of God. Uncertainty will disappear in the light of God like snow melting in the presence of the summer sun. Once the snow is gone the buds begin to prosper. Once the shadows of uncertainty are removed you will prosper likewise. You will know yourself to be accepted by God. This might sound strange or unbelievable. However, you really can experience it and turn it into your life's reality with all its benefits to know the truth.

Faith is powerful. Trusting in God is powerful: "Trust in the LORD with all thine heart; and lean not unto thine own understanding. In all thy ways acknowledge him, and he shall direct thy paths." (Proverbs 3:5, 6) To put it in a nutshell: God is gracious and merciful and offers eternal life through Jesus Christ. Through faith you receive Jesus, which means to believe in him and accept him as Lord and Savior.

> Faith has an originator. It is God himself.

Jesus promises "that whosoever believeth in him should not perish, but have everlasting life." (John 3:16) There is no doubt about it. The Apostle Paul puts it this way: "For I am not ashamed of the gospel of Christ: for it is the power of God unto salvation to every one that believeth; to the Jew first, and also to the Greek." (Romans 1:16) The Gospel of

Jesus Christ is the power *of God* that saves the one who believes. It is not your own power at all but the power of God that saves you and transforms your entire life into a life full of joy, happiness, and true freedom.

You do not need to earn the right to receive truth, eternal life, and peace of mind. You simply need to receive what God has already provided for you and for me, in Christ. You do not need to walk in darkness anymore, but instead, you can live a life in the light and grace of God by receiving Christ through faith.

Receiving Christ—no theory, but reality

God lets you know the way, the truth, and the life. It is Jesus Christ. So far, parts of what has been mentioned might somehow seem to be very abstract. Nothing could be farther from the truth than faith being abstract or a mere theoretical construct. Receiving Christ is not a theoretical matter. Knowing the truth is also not a theoretical matter. These aspects are promises of God himself. In the previous paragraphs we discussed how to receive Christ. It is through faith that you can accept Christ in your life. And your faith is a consequence of hearing the word of God. Once you have found Jesus Christ, "the way, the truth, and the life" (John 14:6), you will be set free. Remember the words of Jesus in this verse: "no man cometh unto the Father, but by me." (John 14:6) Finding Jesus is the key to perfect peace and personal freedom. This is certainly true and not plain theory.

How can you find Jesus and get to know the truth? How can you switch from purely knowing *about* Jesus Christ and being solely familiar with all the things belonging to him to the level of knowing him personally? It is not a matter of knowing the truth from hearsay, but knowing the truth by personal experience and an encounter with the Lord Jesus Christ.

The Bible tells us about many people who have had an encounter with Jesus. It even happens today! Lives have been changed. Their thinking and behaviors have been transformed. Here is a short illustration on theory vs. experience: Imagine you have an apple in your right hand. You observe it. You know that it is an apple. You can even find reports on what this apple tastes like and what it would feel like in your mouth.

> It is not a complex endeavor to find the truth.

But you do not have experience actually eating it yet. You know everything about the apple and its potential taste, in theory. Still, you are not sure about its taste and continue to observe it. In this state of uncertainty you are vulnerable to deception. People are able to influence your opinion about the apple. They could possibly tell you all kinds of stories, and even direct your thoughts in the direction of their own desires.

Thus, if they want to hinder you from eating this apple, they will put effort into finding confirmations that would lead you to stop wanting to eat the apple. On the contrary, they will tell great stories about the delicious taste if they want you to eat the apple. They could simply play ping-pong with you, because you are still in a state of uncertainty, only assuming what the taste of the apple is. But, what happens if you actually eat the apple? You simply know what it is like to eat the apple. You know its taste. Nobody can easily deceive you anymore, because the taste, the smell, and everything about the apple is now entwined with your personal experience.

Now, what is the point of this illustration? If you do not know the truth personally, others can tell you to do this and that, to believe this and that, and to think in this or that direction. You are vulnerable to deceptions and highly likely to be influenced by what others may say or believe. You are in a state of uncertainty.

Therefore, Jesus says that you need to receive him personally. It is not enough just to know about Christ and some subjects in religion. You need to have a personal encounter with him! Indeed, knowing Jesus is not a theoretical issue at all. "Ask, and it shall be given you; seek, and ye shall find; knock, and it shall be opened unto you: for every one that asketh receiveth; and he that seeketh findeth; and to him that knocketh it shall be opened." (Matthew 7:7, 8) Jesus promises that you will find, once you seek; that you will receive, once you ask; that the door to the spiritual world will be opened to you, once you knock. If you dare!

Seeking, receiving, and so on, these actions are expressing your very wish to know the truth. And there is no doubt that you will receive it. If you are honestly approaching Jesus and asking him to come into your life and enter your heart, he assures you that "the one who comes to Me I will by no means cast out." (John 6:37) This is the very promise of Jesus Christ.

Having received Jesus in your heart, your life and way of thinking will be transformed, and you will not only know *about* Jesus and his promises, but you will literally *know* him. This very personal experience and encounter with the Lord Jesus Christ is called spiritual regeneration. It will be your personal experience, far from being a theoretical matter.

God lets you know how to receive Jesus and have a

personal encounter with him. It is not tricky or a complex endeavor to find the truth. Jesus actually wants you to find him. Jesus says: "Behold, I stand at the door, and knock: if any man hear my voice, and open the door, I will come in to him, and will sup with him, and he with me." (Revelation 3:20)

He stands before the door of your heart and knocks. Jesus will not just kick in your door and force himself and his gift of eternal life and truth on you. This is surely not his approach nor attitude. He wants you to love him unconditionally, and primarily, voluntarily. So it is up to you to either open the door and invite Jesus in, or let the door remain closed. I want to warmly encourage you to dare to let Jesus in!

Spiritual regeneration—being born again

God lets you know the impact of spiritual regeneration. Let us be quite clear, in biblical terms, spiritual regeneration has nothing to do with reincarnation or alike concepts. It is rather a divine miracle that completely transforms your life, in particular the spiritual part of who you are. Jesus himself talks about spiritual regeneration and uses the term *to be born again.*

He says that "except a man be born again, he cannot see the kingdom of God." (John 3:3) Being born again means to be a new creature in Christ. This, in turn, implies you are a partaker of the divine nature, and likewise, a child of God.

Nevertheless, God honestly tells you the consequences of not being born again, namely being excluded from eternal life. If you will not see the kingdom of God, it is because you are spiritually blind. Being spiritually blind implies uncertainty. You are literally in the dark. Again, being in the dark tells you that you are not in the light. Therefore, it is essential to be truly born again in order to see the kingdom of God and be able to enter into it.

Spiritual regeneration is in fact receiving Christ through faith and transcending from death to life. The life of a born-again person is now under the sovereignty of Christ. This is reality, not science fiction or anything abstract. You can take it literally. If you have not personally experienced the spiritual regeneration, you probably cannot even imagine the reality of it. But I guarantee you that you will see clearly once you have found the truth that is Jesus Christ himself. Jesus encourages you to open your heart and let him show you *the* reality of life.

Remember, it is absurd to think salvation is dependent on what you *do*. Absolutely unreasonable! Instead, I remind you of the very words of Jesus Christ. He died for the sins of the world so "that whosoever believeth in him should not perish, but have everlasting life." (John 3:16) It is all about Jesus Christ. Spiritual regeneration happens if you devote yourself to God. Spiritual regeneration comes to pass because you believe in Jesus Christ and his work of redemption.

> Being born again is like transcending from death to life. Unless you believe, you cannot see the spiritual reality around you.

In addition, Jesus mentions another essential aspect in the context of being born again: "Verily, verily, I say unto thee, Except a man be born of water and *of* the Spirit, he cannot enter into the kingdom of God." (John 3:5) Before we have a look at the meaning of "born of the Spirit," let us derive the meaning of the water in the context of spiritual regeneration. In the episode with the woman of Samaria at Jacob's well, Jesus asked her to give him something to drink. The woman was surprised that a Jew was talking to her, a Samaritan woman. Thereupon, Jesus answered "and said unto her, If thou knewest the gift of God, and who it is that saith to thee, Give me to drink; thou wouldest have asked of him, and he would have given thee living water." (John 4:10) Jesus tells the woman that he would have given her *living* water if she had merely asked for. By the way, he affirms the principle of "ask, and it shall be given you." (Matthew 7:7) Anyhow, the woman did not understand the spiritual meaning behind the statement of Jesus. She was wondering how Jesus could provide water without anything to draw with. Then she asked Jesus if he is greater than Jacob, who gave them the well they were standing at right then. Now let us focus on Jesus' answer to this question: "Jesus answered and said unto her, 'Whosoever drinketh of this water shall thirst again: but whosoever drinketh of the water that I shall give him shall never thirst; but the water that I shall give him shall be in him a well of water springing up into everlasting life.' " (John 4:13, 14).

> Jesus is the well of living water. And once received, you will never thirst again. It is sufficient to stop your spiritual thirst.

The water that originates from Jacob's well does not satisfy thirst. On the contrary, Jesus will provide water that absolutely satisfies thirst. There is a deep meaning behind this statement. It tells you that even Jacob's water is not comparable with the living water of Christ. Jacob was under the old covenant, and the message of the old covenant was not satisfying and vivid, nor complete, because it was only "a shadow of things to come." (Colossians 2:17) Whereas Jesus was the substance and originator of the new covenant, and so the message of Jesus was sufficient and complete in itself. As a consequence, if you drink from the living water Jesus is offering, you will never thirst again.

Being born of water

The living water is able to satisfy your thirst for true knowledge. Now, what is the water Jesus is talking about? It is the holy Spirit, of whom Jesus said, "I will send unto you from the Father." (John 15:26) When you are spiritually born again, you receive Christ, but you also receive the holy Spirit.

Jesus describes the holy Spirit as follows: "But the Comforter, which is the Holy Ghost, whom the Father will send in my name, he shall teach you all things, and bring all things to your remembrance, whatsoever I have said unto you." (John 14:26) The holy Spirit undertakes a crucial part in the spiritual regeneration of a person who seeks God wholeheartedly.

The holy Spirit and the spiritual regeneration

It is the holy Spirit who "will guide you into all truth: for he shall not speak of himself; but whatsoever he shall hear, that shall he speak: and he will shew you things to come." (John 16:13) The holy Spirit is sent by Jesus to guide you in your life. Through the spiritual regeneration, you receive the Spirit of adoption, in contrast to the spirit of bondage unto fear. Now this is crucial in the context of freedom of uncertainty. Through the holy Spirit, you now know the truth, and the truth sets you free. Free from bondage, free from fear, free from uncertainty, and free from a limited degree of freedom.

The Apostle Paul formulates it this way: "For ye have not received the spirit of bondage again to fear; but ye have received the Spirit of adoption, whereby we cry, Abba, Father. The Spirit itself beareth witness with our spirit, that we are the children of God: And if children, then heirs; heirs of God, and joint-heirs with Christ." (Romans 8:15-17) With God there is no room for uncertainty. If you are a child of God, you are an heir. If you are an heir, you are a joint-heir with Christ. These are words of encouragement and assurance from a God, who loves you unconditionally!

> Having been born again, you received the Spirit of adoption. You are a child of the living God.

Being born of the Spirit

Jesus says that you will not enter into the kingdom of God unless you are born of water and of the Spirit. We have seen that the living water is the holy Spirit. But what does it mean to be born of the Spirit? It is the holy Spirit that gets in contact with your spirit. "The Spirit itself beareth witness with our spirit, that we are the children of God." (Romans 8:16) It is the holy Spirit telling your spirit that you are a child of God.

Thus, spiritual regeneration is not taking place on a mere rational, but rather on a spiritual level. Hence, "being born of the Spirit" means that both your spirit and the holy Spirit are involved in this process of regeneration. It is not your own understanding and level of rational thinking abilities that bear witness, but it is the holy Spirit bearing witness with your spirit. "Trust in the LORD with all thine heart; and lean not unto thine own understanding." (Proverbs 3:5) You need to fully put your trust in God. This is certainly true and worth remembering. To define it concisely: spiritual regeneration is receiving Christ through faith. You experience it on a spiritual level, where the holy Spirit bears witness with your spirit, telling you: you *are* a child of God!

The impact of being born of water and of the Spirit

Once you have received Christ, the scales will fall from your eyes, and you will be able to see clearly. As a child of God, no one needs to teach you anymore how to know God "for they shall all know me, from the least of them unto the greatest of them, saith the LORD: for I will forgive their iniquity, and I will remember their sin no more." (Jeremiah 31:34) This is an explicit message from Jeremiah, God's prophet, pointing to the promised Messiah and his new covenant.

Moreover, as a child of God, you *hear* the words of God as it is prophesied: "He that is of God heareth God's words: ye therefore hear them not, because ye are not of God." (John 8:47) In this context, the verb to hear may also mean to *understand* in the Greek original text. Thus, a child of God will understand the words of God. The reason why the majority of mankind does not hear God's word is because people are not born again. They are not children of God and have not yet experienced the spiritual regeneration. In Christ, however, a person is a child of God, and therefore a new creature, born again and dwelling in his presence. To be in the truth means to be in the light: no fear, but assured freedom galore.

Receiving eternal life . . . but when?

So far, we have seen that eternal life is a gift of God for

everyone. But only those who have been born again of water and of the Spirit will receive it. The following question remains open: when do you actually receive eternal life?

In the Christian community, you can find a wide variety of answers to the question of when a child of God receives eternal life. There are some who think eternal life will be given to believers in Christ as a byproduct of receiving Jesus into their lives. Others may believe that it is conferred on believers at Christ's return.

Both views are somehow true, but only to a certain extent. If we do not know the truth, we will not receive true knowledge. Not knowing the truth automatically introduces uncertainty, which is not God's will for mankind. But thanks to God, He lets you know the time a person receives eternal life: "In a moment, in the twinkling of an eye, at the last trump: for the trumpet shall sound,

> At Christ's return a born-again person will be freed from mortality.

and the dead shall be raised incorruptible, and we shall be changed, for this corruptible must put on incorruption, and this mortal must put on immortality. So when this corruptible shall have put on incorruption, and this mortal shall have put on immortality, then shall be brought to pass the saying that is written, Death is swallowed up in victory." (1 Corinthians 15:52-54)

At the last trumpet before Christ's imminent return, those who have already died in Christ will be raised incorruptible. Those who are born again and still alive at Christ's return will be changed, from being corruptible to being incorruptible and from being mortal to being immortal. Being immortal means to die no more, which is to live forever. At Christ's return, a born-again follower of Christ will put on immortality. It is then that mortality is obviously taken off completely.

Besides this, John lets us know that all his words he wrote down in his letters serve one purpose: "that ye may know that ye have eternal life, and that ye may believe on the name of the Son of God." (1 John 5:13) He addresses those who believe in Jesus and encourages them anew to believe on the name of Jesus Christ. In the same breath, John eradicates every doubt about whether they who believe on the name of Jesus have eternal life or not. Surely, those who believe have eternal life.

They may be in a mortal body, but they nevertheless have eternal life. Although you will put on immortality only at Christ's return, you have already received the gift of God that is eternal life in Christ. This is by no means a contradiction. It is mortality that will be put off from you when Christ returns. Till then you are sealed within a mortal body, but having the assurance of being saved by grace through faith. Paul affirms: "Who hath also sealed us, and given the earnest of the Spirit in our hearts." (2 Corinthians 1:22) God seals you by gifting the earnest of the Spirit in your heart.

The holy Spirit: the seal of God

The holy Spirit is not only the earnest till the day of Christ's return, but he himself is also the seal of God. "And grieve not the holy Spirit of God, whereby ye are sealed unto the day of redemption." (Ephesians 4:30) By spiritual regeneration, a change in sovereignty in your life will happen. You pass from death to eternal life. The earnest for eternal life is the holy Spirit. Indeed, it is God who seals you with his Spirit unto the day of redemption. It is He who provides for your eternal destiny. Your part in this spiritual transformation process is simply to stretch out and receive! The eternal destiny of each and every person on this planet Earth will then finally be consolidated at Christ's return.

Christ's return, when is it?

When Jesus returns there will be no further possibility to decide on which path you want to go: be it the way of darkness or the way of light. God lets you know that Christ's return will put an end to the world you now know. It will introduce the closing scene of this earth's history.

But when will Christ actually return? There is no scriptural evidence on the date of Christ's return. Quite the contrary, Jesus points out: "Watch therefore, for ye know neither the day nor the hour wherein the Son of man cometh." (Matthew 25:13) Nobody knows the day nor the hour, "but my Father only" (Matthew 24:36) says the Lord Jesus Christ. This knowledge helps us to be absolutely sure that a human person will never know the day or hour of Christ's return. It is the heavenly Father who knows it exclusively.

Hence, if someone is proclaiming a date for Jesus' return, you can be sure that "the prophet hath spoken it presumptuously: thou shalt not be afraid of him." (Deuteronomy 18:22) You do not need to be afraid of this false prophet. In other words, you do not need to have fear in any respect. The box of uncertainty need not be opened. Just remember, the heavenly Father knows the exact time of *the* upcoming most historic event in the history of mankind. God is in control.

Signs of Christ's imminent return

God lists several signs indicating the imminent return of the Lord Jesus Christ. Basically, in the Gospel according to Luke you find an illustrative description about what it will be like when Jesus literally returns. Jesus compares the days of Noah with the day when Jesus, the Son of man, comes back the second time: "And as it was in the days of Noe, so shall it be also in the days of the Son of man. They did eat, they drank, they married wives, they were given in marriage, until the day that Noe entered into the ark, and the flood came, and destroyed them all." (Luke 17:26, 27) Noah was truly a man of faith. After God had given him the incredible task to build an ark to save his family, including himself, Noah immediately started to build the ark according to God's instructions.

In Noah's time the earth was filled with violence, adultery, idolatry, and many more negative manifestations of mankind. Do you recognize the obvious parallels to the manifold manifestations of evil in current times? God pronounced the verdict: "And God said unto Noah, 'The end of all flesh is come before me; for the earth is filled with violence through them; and, behold, I will destroy them with the earth.' " (Genesis 6:13) Noah was entrusted with this message of judgment. Was God's move unfair or unjust? Not at all! Why? Because God warned of his intention beforehand, and the people could have made the decision to follow the path of light in order to escape death. As it is written: "Surely the Lord GOD will do nothing, but he revealeth his secret unto his servants the prophets." (Amos 3:7) God kept his word then, and he will also keep it in the future.

> In the times of Noah, being in the ark meant to be saved. Today, being in Christ means to be saved.

God is patient. "Which sometime were disobedient, when once the longsuffering of God waited in the days of Noah, while the ark was a preparing, wherein few, that is, eight souls were saved by water." (1 Peter 3:20) The people of that time of Noah had the chance to literally get on board of the ark. Yet only eight people got saved. The people did not listen to God's warnings. At least, they did not take heed of that holy warning.

Nowadays people have the opportunity to spiritually get on board as well. The ark, metaphorically speaking, is nothing less than Jesus Christ himself. How were Noah and his family saved? They believed in God and acted upon his order accordingly. How could you be saved? If you believe in Jesus and, as a consequence, act upon his order by faith! Being in the ark saved the people in the times of Noah. Analogously, being in Christ and believing in his name will save you.

In the times of Noah, besides doing evil, the people were also eating, drinking, and marrying. These activities are not evil in themselves, but that is not the point of the true message of this statement. Rather, it indicates that people will be so preoccupied with their daily duties in life that they will finally forget their heavenly Creator. They will not "watch and pray." (Matthew 26:41) They neither will listen to God and his messengers. Christ's return, and thus God's judgment, "will come as a thief in the night" (2 Peter 3:10) for those who do not believe.

In conclusion, there are two lessons to be learned from

the whole story, and these are precious hints concerning Christ's return. First, the earth will be filled with violence and evil people who do not believe in God anymore. Second, the world will be extremely distracted from the truth by mere conventional activities, like eating and drinking. Are these signs already visible in today's society? Noah's contemporaries rejected God's clear invitation and willingly refused to enter the ark—and they all died. How will you respond to God's invitation? Will *you* get on board and be saved by God's grace?

A place being prepared before Christ's return

God wants us to be prepared for the great day of the Lord Jesus Christ. We do not know the exact hour when Jesus will visibly come a second time. What we do know is that he will come to take the believers to a place where he is. Jesus once said: "And if I go and prepare a place for you, I will come again, and receive you unto myself; that where I am, there ye may be also." (John 14:3) What a wonderful promise! Jesus is preparing a place for us in the house of the heavenly Father. We can trust in his word, because God does not lie. "God is not a man, that he should lie." (Numbers 23:19) His words are true. After his ascension, Jesus actually has not left his followers alone. The Gospel according to Matthew ends with an encouraging message from the words of the Lord and Savior of the world: "I am with you always, even unto the end of the world." (Matthew 28:20) Jesus has never left us alone.

He further promised: "I will not leave you comfortless: I will come to you." (John 14:18) Through the holy Spirit, Jesus is always present. "But ye shall receive power, after that the Holy Ghost is come upon you." (Acts 1:8) The promised

Spirit of God is poured out into our hearts if we receive Christ. Thus, while we are waiting till Christ visibly returns to take his people and bring them into the heavenly mansions, we know that Jesus is with us through the holy Spirit. We are not left alone!

However, believers in Jesus Christ long for the return of their beloved Savior to literally embrace their Creator and Redeemer. But how will this historic occasion of Christ's return take place? Will it be in secrecy, only for his chosen people? Will it be visible merely on a certain place on Earth? How will it actually happen? Or has it already taken place?

Christ's return, what will it look like?

God lets you know what Christ's return will look like so that you are protected against deception of all sorts. You will doubtless see that Jesus has not yet returned. The Apostle Paul clearly describes the second coming of Christ in his letter to the Thessalonians. "For the Lord himself shall descend from heaven with a shout, with the voice of the archangel, and with the trump of God: and the dead in Christ shall rise first: then we which are alive and remain shall be caught up together with them in the clouds, to meet the Lord in the air: and so shall we ever be with the Lord." (1 Thessalonians 4:16, 17) The context in which those two verses are mentioned talks about not feeling sorrow concerning those who are asleep, because *those in Christ* will rise on the great day of the coming of Christ.

However, those verses contain some interesting information in particular concerning the second coming of Christ itself: First, Jesus descends from heaven with a shout, with the voice of the archangel and with the trump of God.

This is in harmony with what Paul tells the Corinthians: "In a moment, in the twinkling of an eye, at the last trump: for the trumpet shall sound, and the dead shall be raised incorruptible, and we shall be changed." (1 Corinthians 15:52) Second, the last trump will sound and the *dead in Christ* will rise—this is the so-called resurrection of the dead. Thus, at the coming of Christ, the dead in Christ will rise. The ones who are alive will not precede those who are dead. This implies, by the way, that the dead have not yet joined the Lord. We will examine the state of the dead in more detail later in this chapter. The ones who are alive will be caught up in the clouds together with the dead who are risen.

It is *in the air* where they meet the Lord. This is a very crucial aspect of Christ's return. It answers the previously raised question of whether the second coming of Jesus will be in secrecy.

> When Jesus returns, the living believers will be caught up in the air to meet their Savior and Lord, participating in the first resurrection.

The answer is the following: Jesus will not touch the earth at his second coming. The true followers of Jesus are caught up in the air, and it is *there* they meet their Savior and Lord. Thus, it is deceptive to assume that Jesus will pop up at certain places here and there, showing himself to true believers.

Based on mere written record, we know for certain that the followers of Christ—may they be dead or alive at the coming of Jesus—will meet their Lord in the air. But will this event be visible merely on a specific place on Earth? Surely not. This great happening of the coming of the Lord will be for all to see. John who "bare record of the word of God, and of the testimony of Jesus Christ, and of all things that he saw" (Revelation 1:2) provides notable evidence that all mankind will see Jesus at his second coming. "Behold, he cometh with clouds; and every eye shall see him, and they also which pierced him: and all kindreds of the earth shall wail because of him. Even so, Amen." (Revelation 1:7)

When Jesus comes to take his people to the heavenly places, every eye will see him. At the second coming of Christ, the dead in Christ will rise and will be caught up together with the faithful ones who are alive to meet the Lord in the air. This is called the *first* resurrection. "Blessed and holy is he that hath part in the first resurrection: on such the second death hath no power, but they shall be priests of God and of Christ." (Revelation 20:6)

Those people are saved and will reign with Christ for a thousand years. "And I saw thrones, and they sat upon them, and judgment was given unto them: and I saw the souls of them that were beheaded for the witness of Jesus, and for the word of God, and which had not worshipped the beast, neither his image, neither had received his mark upon their foreheads, or in their hands; and they lived and reigned with Christ a thousand years." (Revelation 20:4)

However, there is a *second* resurrection, which answers the question about where the dead are who did *not* die in Christ and hence did not take part in the first resurrection. The Apostle John provides insight on this matter: "Marvel not at this: for the hour is coming, in which all that are in the graves shall hear his voice, and shall come forth; they that have done good, unto the *resurrection of life*; and they that have done evil, unto the *resurrection of damnation*." (John 5:28, 29) Obviously, the first resurrection is called the resurrection of life and the second is named the resurrection of damnation.

So what about the people who did not die in Christ, thus are still in the graves? John responds: "But the rest of the dead lived not again until the thousand years were finished." (Revelation 20:5) The dead who were not part of the first resurrection remain dead in the graves till a thousand years have gone by. The unconverted people are "not found written in the book of life" (Revelation 20:15) and will participate in the second resurrection which ends up in "the lake of fire. This is the second death." (Revelation 20:14)

So Christ's return is somehow the final point in time which seals your destiny forever. Christ has returned, and after a thousand years, all mankind has been judged accordingly. After the judgment, God makes everything new. John reports it in this way: "And I saw a new heaven and a new earth: for the first heaven and the first earth were passed away; and there was no more sea." (Revelation 21:1) God creates a new earth and a new heaven for his beloved children.

> Believers in Christ have a great view on what will happen after the second coming of Jesus. God makes everything new: no sorrow, no crying, no pain.

Moreover, John continues: "And I, John, saw the holy city, new Jerusalem, coming down from God out of heaven, prepared as a bride adorned for her husband." (Revelation 21:2). The new Jerusalem comes down from God out of heaven. This will be the city the children of God will inherit. There will be no death, no sorrow, nor crying. "God shall wipe away all tears from their eyes; and there shall be no more death, neither sorrow, nor crying, neither shall there be any more pain: for the former things are passed away." (Revelation 21:4) This is good news! This is what you can expect after the second coming of Jesus Christ.

Christ's second coming, in a nutshell

Jesus descends from heaven with the trump of God. He will surely not touch the earth. The ones who died in Christ will rise and be part of the first resurrection, that is the resurrection of life. They will be caught up in the air together with the saints who are alive to meet their Lord and Savior. They will reign a thousand years with Christ. After this period, those who did not believe in Christ will be part of the second resurrection, which is also called the resurrection of damnation. Ultimately, there are two endings: eternal life for those who believe in Christ, or eternal damnation for those who did not receive Christ in their life.

God lets you know the truth. In Christ, God provided everything that you might be saved. Remember, God is good and "will have all men to be saved." (1 Timothy 2:4) He assures you: "As I live, saith the Lord GOD, I have no pleasure in the death of the wicked; but that the wicked turn from his way and live: turn ye, turn ye from your evil ways; for why will ye die?" (Ezekiel 33:11) Catch hold of God's arm and live!

Beyond the veil

So far, we had a look at the spiritual regeneration, eternal life and when we may receive it, Christ's return and its characteristics, and the two types of resurrection. At the coming of the Lord, the dead in Christ will rise. This implies that the dead have not yet been alive. It is implausible to assume that they have already been with the Lord.

Thus, the question on the state of the dead needs to be addressed to remove uncertainty even on that topic. Basically, there are two hypotheses. First, the moment you die, you are with the Lord the very next moment. The second hypothesis is the idea of soul sleep, which implies that you die and remain in the grave asleep till Christ returns. Whatever the wording might be, it must be consistent with God's word.

Therefore, let us deeply examine what happens after we die. But before we have a look at what happens after death, let us first answer the question of where we originally come from.

Beyond the veil: where we come from

In Genesis a detailed report of man's creation is provided: "And the LORD God formed man of the dust of the ground, and breathed into his nostrils the breath of life; and man became a living soul." (Genesis 2:7) We are God's creation. God created you and me. After the process of creation, man became a living *soul*. The term *soul* is often misused to emphasize particular doctrines, for example, the heathen doctrine of the immortality of the soul.

Beyond the veil: the soul and its definition

What is meant by the term soul? In Genesis chapter 2 God provides its simple and unambiguous definition. First you take dust of the ground and form man. Second, you take God's breath of life and put it into the nostrils of this man's form. The result is a living soul. Hence, the equation goes like this: *a living soul = man formed of dust of the ground + God's breath of life*. This is the definition of the term soul itself, nothing more, nothing less. Thus, in order to be a living soul, you need to have two essential ingredients, which are dust and the breath of life. A living soul does not exist unless both components are in place.

<table>
<tr><td>The soul consists of body and spirit which are equivalent to dust and breath of life.</td></tr>
</table>

Beyond the veil: what happens after you die

Now, after having clarified the terminology, we may tackle the core question of what happens after a human being passes away. King Solomon once said: "Then shall the dust return to the earth as it was: and the spirit shall return unto God who gave it." (Ecclesiastes 2:7) Solomon describes the process of dying in explicit terms. The dust, the first element used in the creation process, is the base material of the human being. It returns to the earth as it was in the beginning. This is quite reasonable. The second element of the living soul is the spirit that returns to God. Notice, it is not the soul returning to God, but it is the spirit instead. The Psalmist David puts it this way: "Thou hidest thy face, they are troubled: thou takest away their breath, they die, and return to their dust." (Psalms 104:29) Again, we have the two elements, the dust and the breath. If you die, dust gets separated from the breath. The soul is not a *living* soul anymore.

As previously mentioned, Solomon said that the spirit will return to God after someone passes away. Now, what is the spirit mentioned in this context? James, "a servant of God and of the Lord Jesus Christ" (James 1:1) clearly points out that the "body without the spirit is dead." (James 2:26) Also,

Job was aware of what kept him alive: "All the while my breath is in me, and the spirit of God is in my nostrils." (Job 27:3) Comparing the mentioned viewpoints of Solomon, James, and Job with the statement of Moses in Genesis 2:7, ask yourself what God breathed into the nostrils of Adam, formed of the dust of the ground. It was the breath of life that originated from God himself! Job calls the breath of life simply the spirit of God in man's nostrils. James proclaims that the body without the spirit is dead. Remember that the body is the first and the spirit is the second part of the living soul. Both parts are necessary to be alive. Putting those individual pieces together reminds us of the equation of a living soul. Now, it says: *living soul = body + spirit*. What is the body? It is dust of the ground formed by God. And what is the spirit? It is the breath of life that originates from God himself.

Let us shortly elaborate that the spirit according to this context is the breath of life. We heard that "the spirit shall return unto God who gave it." (Ecclesiastes 12:7) What has God, in fact, given man to be a living soul? It was exactly the breath of life. Furthermore, Job claimed to be alive as long as the spirit of God is in his nostrils. A similar statement is found in Genesis 2:7, where it is reported that God breathed the breath of life into the nostrils of man. The result was that man became a living soul. Comparing these statements of Solomon and Job results in the following conclusion: the spirit that returns to God is the breath of life which has its origin in God. Without the spirit of God, the breath of life, man is just dust of the ground without life in it. This conclusion is consistent with the convictions of the biblical authors Moses, James, Job, and Solomon.

<blockquote>There is no such thing as immortality of the soul.</blockquote>

Beyond the veil: soul and its mortality

Knowing what happens after someone dies, what would consequently be the answer to the question, is it possible for a soul to actually die? The answer is a resounding *yes*, without any uncertainty. The famous quotation of the Apostle Paul has already been quoted several times: "For the wages of sin is death; but the gift of God is eternal life through Jesus Christ our Lord." (Romans 6:23) Not receiving Christ is equivalent to rejecting the gift of God, which is eternal life. The consequence of not receiving the gift of God is death. Remember, without accepting Christ, you are not a partaker of the divine nature. Therefore, you are still in your sins. And, again, the wages of sin is death. There is no exception.

The consequence of sin is death, which refers to the second death, which is "the lake of fire." (Revelation 20:14) Listen to the universal law of life and non-divine nature, respectively: "And as it is appointed unto men once to die, but after this the judgment." (Hebrews 9:27) You only find eternal life in Christ. Rejecting Jesus is equivalent to refusing to accept the gift of eternal life. As a consequence you cannot live forever, but will surely die. Ezekiel the priest gets to the heart of it: "The soul that sinneth, it shall die." (Ezekiel 18:20) This verse does not need further explanation.

Since the Fall of Man the soul has been subject to death. There is only one exceptional scenario in which someone does not die both the natural and the spiritual death: those who believe in Christ and are still alive at Christ's second coming will not die.

In conclusion, confusion is caused by misusing the term soul. In essence, it is simply a question of its definition. The soul is made up of a body formed of dust of the ground and the breath of life, which is the spirit of God. Hence, it is obvious that a soul may die because the "body without the spirit is dead." (James 2:26) You take away one of the "ingredients" of the soul, and you immediately cease to be a living soul.

> Only God has immortality. We do not have it. Only in Christ are we heirs of eternal life.

By the way, it has already been mentioned that it is God "who only hath immortality." (1 Timothy 6:16) Without Christ you have a sinful nature by default. But if you receive Christ, you have been born again, and thus are a new creature and partaker of the divine nature, so to say. "Then Jesus said unto them, 'Verily, verily, I say unto you, Except ye eat the flesh of the Son of man, and drink his blood, ye have no life in you. Whoso eateth my flesh, and drinketh my blood, hath eternal life; and I will raise him up at the last day.' " (John 6:52, 53) You do not have life in you, unless you receive Christ in your heart.

Beyond the veil: immortality and Satan's first lie

It is no coincidence that the soul and its nature are a tough and controversial issue in today's society, in particular within religious institutions. It was Satan's first lie to mankind: "And the serpent said unto the woman, 'Ye shall not surely die.' " (Genesis 3:4) The serpent was Satan himself. "And the great dragon was cast out, that old serpent, called the Devil, and Satan, which deceiveth the whole world: he was cast out into the earth, and his angels were cast out with him." (Revelation 12:9)

God told Adam and Eve not to eat from the tree of knowing good and evil, otherwise they would die. However, Satan precisely addressed this very command of God and successfully tried to convince Adam and Eve to eat the fruit of this tree, nonetheless. At the end, did Adam and Eve have to die? Yes, they did. Who was right and telling the truth? It was God, not the originator of the lie!

Even today religious groups and churches want to deceive you and even lie to you concerning the matter of immortality of the soul. They tell you that you will not die, but have everlasting life *in yourself*. But God is honest with you, and therefore, he lets you know that only *in Christ* is eternal life regained, restoring what Adam and Eve once lost. The truth is that once a soul dies, the body returns to dust where it came from, and the spirit, which is the breath of life, returns to God. At his second coming Christ will wake up the believer.

Beyond the veil: being with the Lord

The spirit returns to God. However, does it mean that you will immediately be with the Lord after you die? Certainly not. The spirit is not a living soul, but the life-giving breath of God. Nevertheless, many Christians believe that once you die you are with the Lord *right away*.

As proof, Jesus' assuring words to one of the malefactors on the cross are cited: "And Jesus said unto him, 'Verily I say unto thee, To day shalt thou be with me in paradise.' " (Luke 23:43) In the first instance it seems that Jesus promised him to be in paradise after he had died. Is it really true? No, it is not. The malefactor was not in paradise on the day he died. And no, Jesus did not lie to him. How does it fit together? Let us have a closer look at the statement in Luke 23:43.

John tells us that Jesus has not yet been with the Father *after* his resurrection: "Jesus saith unto her, 'Touch me not; for I am not yet ascended to my Father: but go to my brethren, and say unto them, I ascend unto my Father, and your Father; and to my God, and your God.' " (John 20:17) Note that Jesus was dead, having been in the grave for three days before he was raised from the dead. Thus, Jesus could not have been in paradise with the

> After his death, Jesus was not with his heavenly Father, but in the grave for three days.

malefactor on the very day they died. Only if the paradise Jesus was talking about is a place where the heavenly Father is not present, then, hypothetically, this could be the case, that Jesus and the malefactor met right there. However, this hypothesis of the existence of two paradises is not confirmed anywhere throughout the entire Bible. But did Jesus lie to the malefactor? Surely not! Let us investigate even further.

In comparison to the English language, there is no such equivalent punctuation in the Greek used at the time when the New Testament was written. So the statement of Jesus could have been equally translated this way as well: "And Jesus said unto him, 'Verily I say unto thee today, thou shalt be with me in paradise.' " (Luke 23:43) Do you notice the difference? It is in the punctuation. Consequently, the semantics of the statement of Jesus has now drastically changed. It now does not implicate anymore that the malefactor and Jesus went to the heavenly Father immediately after they died.

Considering the context of the death and resurrection of Christ, the word "today" cannot relate to the part of the sentence that talks about being in paradise on the same day Jesus and the malefactor died. This meaning simply contradicts the very statement of Jesus to Mary Magdalene: "Touch me not; for I am not yet ascended to my Father." (John 20:17) So even at the level of grammar, it is by no means a supportive argument for the idea of being with the Lord immediately after a person's death.

There is even another biblical report people use as proof that a person is with Christ immediately after having died. It is the parable of the rich man and Lazarus. In the light of what has been said so far, Lazarus and the rich man did not necessarily go to heaven and hell immediately after they had died. It is said: "And it came to pass, that the beggar died, and was carried by the angels into Abraham's bosom: the rich man also died, and was buried." (Luke 16:22)

As mentioned earlier, those who are in Christ will be caught up in the air to meet their Savior. Likewise, Lazarus was carried by the angels into Abraham's bosom. "Marvel not at this: for the hour is coming, in the which all that are in the graves shall hear his voice, and shall come forth; they that have done good, unto the resurrection of life; and they that have done evil, unto the resurrection of damnation." (John 5:28, 29) When do we physically and visibly meet our Lord? It will be at Christ's return, when the dead in the graves shall hear the voice of Jesus. *Then* the dead shall come forth. This truth applies to the parable of the rich man and Lazarus in the same manner.

As a side note, parables are figurative stories. They

certainly reflect important messages, but they are not necessarily to be taken literally. For example, the message behind the parable of Lazarus and the rich man primarily focuses on the fact that people have everything they need for them to be able to trust in God and surrender to Jesus Christ. And the parable tells us that it is not possible to convince people who *do not want* to believe in God, even if someone would raise from the dead. This is the focus of this parable, and it fits its context.

Beyond the veil: the dead know nothing

If the soul, or at least its spirit, is not found with the Lord immediately after you die, where is it in the meantime? Through the words of King Solomon, God lets you know the state of the dead: "For the living know that they shall die: but the dead know not any thing, neither have they any more a reward; for the memory of them is forgotten. Also their love, and their hatred, and their envy, is now perished; neither have they any more a portion for ever in any thing that is done under the sun." (Ecclesiastes 9:5, 6) A characteristic of the dead is obviously to know nothing.

Furthermore, the Psalmist David puts it this way: "The dead praise not the LORD, neither any that go down into silence." (Psalms 115:17) The dead do not even praise the Lord when they die, simply because they are dead. If someone who dies was immediately with the Lord, do you think that this person would stop praising the Lord? By no means! As a matter of fact, David continues: "His breath goeth forth, he returneth to his earth; in that very day his thoughts perish." (Psalms 146:4) Even the thoughts cease to exist.

Death is often referred to as sleep. For instance, Jesus mentioned that Lazarus was sleeping: "these things said he: and after that he saith unto them, 'Our friend Lazarus sleepeth; but I go, that I may awake him out of sleep.' " (John 11:11) But some verses later Jesus said: "Lazarus is dead." (John 11:14) Actually, Lazarus "had lain in the grave four days already." (John 11:17)

In the discussion with Jesus about Lazarus, Martha, the sister of Lazarus, was convinced that her brother would rise in the resurrection of life. "I know that he shall rise again in the resurrection at the last day." (John 11:24) Martha obviously understood that the dead would rise again in the resurrection at the last day, which is pointing to the second coming of Christ.

Another example of death referred to as sleep is the statement of the Psalmist David: "Consider and hear me, O LORD my God: lighten mine eyes, lest I sleep the sleep of death." (Psalms 13:3) He is connecting the word sleep with death. Even the Apostle Paul tried to comfort the followers of Christ in Thessalonica. He promised them that all who believed in Jesus and had passed away were asleep until the great day of the Lord, where Jesus Christ will wake them up again: "But I would not have you to be ignorant, brethren, concerning them which are asleep, that ye sorrow not, even as others which have no hope. For if we believe that Jesus died and rose again, even so them also which sleep in Jesus will God bring with him. For this we say unto you by the word of the Lord, that we which are alive and remain unto the coming of the Lord shall not prevent them which are asleep. For the Lord himself shall descend from heaven with a shout, with the voice of the archangel, and with the trump of God: and the dead in Christ shall rise first: Then we which are alive and remain shall be caught up together with them in the clouds, to meet the Lord in the air: and so shall we ever be with the Lord." (1 Thessalonians 4:13-17) From this statement it is not possible to infer that those who die will immediately be with the Lord after having died.

> Whoever has the Son has life. Whoever does not have the Son of God does not have life.

Moreover, Paul continues: "Behold, I shew you a mystery; We shall not all sleep, but we shall all be changed, in a moment, in the twinkling of an eye, at the last trump: for the trumpet shall sound, and the dead shall be raised incorruptible, and we shall be changed. For this corruptible must put on incorruption, and this mortal must put on immortality." (1 Corinthians 15:51-53) Yes, the transformation will be in the twinkling of an eye. But this will not take place when a believer dies, but it will happen at the last trump after Jesus has come again.

Both passages are absolutely consistent with each other concerning the topic of death and the state of the dead. In conclusion, those who are dead are said to be asleep. And those who are asleep will rise again when the last trump of God will sound with great power at Christ's return. There is no doubt about it. All uncertainty concerning death and afterlife vanishes in the light of Jesus. Christ "hath abolished death, and hath brought life and immortality to light through the gospel." (2 Timothy 1:10) In Jesus you are able to grasp the truth, and it is he who enabled us to embrace life and immortality by *his* death and resurrection. "God commendeth his love toward us, in that, while we were yet sinners, Christ died for us. Much more then, being now justified by his blood, we shall be saved from wrath through him. For if, when we were enemies, we were reconciled to God by the death of his Son, much more, being reconciled, we shall be saved by his life." (Romans 5:8-10) This is the Gospel of Jesus Christ! To *him* be praise and honor and glory, forever!

Personal addendum

I warmly invite you to search the Scriptures by *yourself*. "They received the word with all readiness of mind, and searched the scriptures daily, whether those things were so." (Acts 17:11) The word of God is constant and will not change. Jesus assures you: "heaven and earth shall pass away, but my words shall not pass away." (Matthew 24:35) Approach God, "who will have all men to be saved, and to come unto the knowledge of the truth" (1 Timothy 2:4) and trust in his promise: "and ye shall seek me, and find me, when ye shall search for me with all your heart." (Jeremiah 29:13) It is not a matter of knowing the truth from hearsay or being merely familiar with Jesus and his message, but of knowing the truth after having a personal encounter with the Lord Jesus Christ.

God lets you know that once you have found and received Jesus Christ, the way, the truth, and the life, you will never thirst again, but will come to rest. If you have not yet found this very peace of mind in Christ, heed the gentle call of Jesus: "Come unto me, all ye that labour and are heavy laden, and I will give you rest." (Matthew 11:28) This is Christ's invitation. This is his free gift. This is reality, my friend.

3: The Assurance Of Salvation

To know not means to assume, to assume means to know not. This is the equation of the vicious cycle of uncertainty. The number of manifestations of uncertainty in one's life is almost infinite. These evidences range from distorted self-esteem, unhappiness, ingratitude, and a feeling of spiritually not being at home, to minor and major depressions, thoughts of suicide, and mental ill-health in general. At their root, they are the result of not knowing the truth. It is as simple as that.

Remember the words of Jesus: "And ye shall know the truth, and the truth shall make you free." (John 8:32) This is a powerful statement of assurance. There are no special requirements in order to be set free. You do not have to do this or that to gain freedom, especially spiritual freedom, but it is, so to say, a *two-step process*. First, you need to know the truth. Second, you will be set free by the truth. Notice, it is formulated in a passive voice. It is not you who sets you free, but you will be set free *by the truth*. Your part is to receive the means by which you will be set free. In this process, it is not your part to try to free yourself.

Thus, the element that sets you free is the truth. Now please listen carefully: the truth is not some*thing*, but some*one*. It is Jesus Christ himself. He proclaims to be "the way, the truth, and the life." (John 14:6) If you receive Jesus, you will surely not abide in darkness. Follow the two-step process!

> Spiritual progress does not start with any church membership. It begins with knowing the truth: Jesus.

First step to spiritual freedom

The first step in the two-step process to spiritual freedom is to know the truth. It is not only the first but simultaneously also the *key step* to gaining victory in your spiritual life. It is where the story of spiritual success begins. In contrast, it does not start with any church membership, penitential exercises, or the like. The story of spiritual progress has its start exclusively in knowing the truth. It begins when you know Jesus Christ, and hence, God.

By knowing Jesus you know the heavenly Father as well. Jesus puts it this way: "no man cometh unto the Father, but by me." (John 14:6) Also, "he that hath seen me hath seen the Father." (John 14:9) Furthermore, Jesus says: "I and my Father are one." (John 10:30) Thus, once you have seen and received Jesus, the Son of God, you also have seen and received God, the Father.

How can you receive Jesus? It is *through faith* that you receive the Savior of the world into your life. Receiving is the opposite of refusing or rejecting the gift of God that he is generously offering to mankind. To receive means to give Jesus access to your life. You literally invite Jesus in. He is already patiently waiting in front of the door of your heart.

Talk to him! Approach Jesus in prayer through faith and ask him to come into your life. Trust in God's promises. And it will surely come to pass! Thousands of people have experienced the transforming power and reality of Jesus in their lives. It is truly not a science-fiction movie to have a personal encounter with Jesus. Rather, it is a reality show!

> A personal encounter with Jesus is not a science-fiction movie, but a reality show!

Second step to spiritual freedom

The second step of this two-step process to spiritual freedom will *naturally* follow the first one. It describes the fact that you will be set free. You may ask: Free from what? The truth, Jesus, will set you free from the bondage of sin and its various manifestations that negatively affect your life. You will see the spiritual world once you know the truth. Sin will not be an abstract term anymore, but it becomes very tangible and particularly real to you. So let us have a closer look at what sin is and how it differs from its plural, sins.

Sin is the root cause of sins

In essence, sin is *the* separating entity between sinful mankind and God. In this context, separation does not mean that God is infinitely far away from his creation or that he does not care about it. As a matter of fact, God *does* care, in that he sent his Son, Jesus Christ, while we were yet sinners, to free us from sin. Remember, the wages of sin is death, in contrast to eternal life. Therefore, separation means that a sinful nature by definition is to receive sin's wages, death. And death without having received Christ in fact literally separates

> Sin is to not believe in Jesus Christ. It is to reject the Savior of the world.

us from eternal life, and likewise from the presence of God. Only through the redemptive work of Jesus Christ is it possible for the believer to escape the consequences of sin, and hence the separation from God. However, in Christ you inherit the gift of salvation by grace through faith.

Sin is the reason why you cannot fully put your trust in God. In fact, sin is to mistrust God and to not believe in Jesus Christ. (John 16:9) Here I am *not* talking about sin*s*, in plural form, but sin, in singular form. Sins are the consequence of sin itself. This is very important to understand: Sin is the root cause of sins. However, sins are the manifestations of sin, so to speak. Therefore, sins are actually not the basic problem in your life, but it is sin itself that separates you from God.

Let me give you an example to illustrate the difference between sin and sins. What would you typically do if you had a terrible headache? Well, there are, of course, several options to deal with this problem. Likely, if you know that there is certain medicine available to ease the pain for your particular problem, you might take that medication accordingly. The symptoms disappear and the medication provides relief, at least for a certain period of time. Surely, you are happy that the pain, the symptom, is gone, but, in fact, the root cause remains untouched. The root cause of the headache, which may be stress, a tumor, or the fact that you simply are not well-hydrated, has not been tackled at all. Thus, the symptoms of your headache might potentially manifest again later in your life. In general, this is what medication aims for:

it fights against the symptoms of the illness, not the illness itself. So, are you really healed by fighting against the symptoms? Definitely not! You actually need to see a doctor who knows about the headache and its potential root causes. The doctor can now clarify if

> Stop fighting against sin's *symptoms*! You need to get rid of sin itself.

these root causes are the reasons for your symptoms and will be able to treat them accordingly. Once the root cause has been eradicated, its symptoms will *automatically* disappear. The person does not need to do anything to treat the pain. Why? Because it is gone, due to the fact that the pain's root cause has been successfully dealt with.

Sin is the root cause, and sins are its symptoms. Jesus is the true doctor and has the power and godly authority to remove sin from your life. Many people try to deal with sin's symptoms, like depression, unhappiness, ingratitude, hatred, envy, adultery, and even more. If they feel depressed or unhappy, chocolate, for instance, seems to be the appropriate drug of choice. What are people actually doing? In essence, they are doing the same as the person with the headache: they are addressing the symptoms, not the root cause itself! Instead of approaching their heavenly doctor and letting him deal with the root cause of their sins, they try to overcome individual sins by their own strength. This is comparable with dealing with the symptoms only! You need to know that you may be able to minimize your manifestations of sin, but it still does not remove sin from your life. You need to get rid of the root cause of your sins. Stop fighting against the symptoms of sin!

Get free from sin!

<blockquote>An encounter with the Lord Jesus Christ will surely open your eyes to see the spiritual reality around you.</blockquote>

You will not get free from all your sins, unless you eradicate their root cause, which is sin itself. In the first place, Jesus promises that he will set you free from the root cause of evil manifestations. After being set free, you will be able to identify the misleading deception that you can remove sin by trying to remove sins. This could not be farther from the truth! First, you can only remove, or at least minimize, certain sins; second, you are absolutely not able to deal with sin itself by yourself.

The Apostle Paul puts it this way: "For what the law could not do, in that it was weak through the flesh, God sending his own Son in the likeness of sinful flesh, and for sin, condemned sin in the flesh." (Romans 8:3) What is this verse telling us about sin? God condemned sin in the flesh through Jesus Christ. It was not possible through the law, or by keeping the law, to condemn sin. "For by grace are ye saved through faith; and that not of yourselves: it is the gift of God: not of works, lest any man should boast." (Ephesians 2:8, 9) You can only be saved from sin through faith in Jesus Christ. It is the gift of God. It is not about you and your own endeavors. At most, your works are like fighting against the symptoms of sin. It is the truth that basically sets you free from sin in every respect of your life.

Jesus heals you and opens your eyes, so that you will see the spiritual reality. Once you have completed the two-step process, you will not only know *about* Jesus, but you will certainly know Jesus literally. You will have had an encounter with your Savior and Lord: this is called the spiritual regeneration, which is often referred to as being born again and being born of water and of the Spirit.

Being born again means to receive Christ through faith. It is a highly spiritual experience. You come to faith and believe in Jesus and his redemptive work that he did for your sake. Then the holy Spirit bears witness with your spirit that you are a child of God and a member of the body of Christ. What is more, in Christ you are a new creature and partaker of the divine nature.

It is essential to understand the relationship between sin and sins. Sins are merely the symptoms of sin. It is Jesus who wants you to be free from the bondage of sin. It is he who has the power and authority to eradicate sin in your life. If you receive Jesus and believe in him, you will for sure experience the spiritual regeneration. You are now able to trust God afresh.

> There is no respect of persons with God; everyone is equally valuable.

God is closer than you might think

"The LORD is nigh unto all them that call upon him, to all that call upon him in truth." (Psalms 145:18) God is trustworthy and keeps his word. If you sincerely call upon him, he will answer your prayer. God "seeth not as man seeth; for man looketh on the outward appearance, but the LORD looketh on the heart." (1 Samuel 16:7) He knows you even before the beginning of your existence: "Before I formed thee in the belly I knew thee." (Jeremiah 1:5)

If you surrender and give your life to Jesus, if you really

want to receive him and invite him into your life, he will reveal himself to you, and you will know the truth. All that has been said so far will not be pure facts and probably unrealistic stories, but your eyes will see the spiritual world and perceive its reality. Let it be assured to you that this book would not have been written as a plain theory without any power or real manifestations in someone's life. Everyone can experience the transforming power of truth. There is no exception.

The Apostle Paul emphasizes that "there is no respect of persons with God." (Romans 2:11) God is not prejudiced against anybody. He loves you and me and the rest of the world. Again, God assures you: "and you will seek Me and find Me, when you search for Me with all your heart." (Jeremiah 29:13)

You need to search for God with all your heart. That is one of the keys to finding Him, a sincere and willing heart. God loves you. He is merciful. However, many people have a distorted image of God that inherently prevents them from approaching God. Fear, which is nothing more than a symptom of uncertainty, rules in and over their entire lives. Uncertainty about God and his character does not strengthen the assurance of salvation we can have in Jesus Christ, but constantly paralyzes and, consequently, prevents us from making progress on our spiritual journey toward God. Therefore, let us examine a couple of attributes of God.

God's attributes: thoughts of peace

The examination of the attributes of God is intended to establish firmly our faith in the one true God who is not against us, but *for* us. Listen to his words: " 'For I know the thoughts that I think toward you', says the LORD, 'thoughts of peace and not of evil, to give you a future and a hope.' " (Jeremiah 29:11) This is what God is thinking about his creation: thoughts of peace, not of evil.

> Love God with all your heart and love your neighbor as yourself. There is no commandment greater than these two.

God's attributes: love

One of the most intrinsic attributes of God is *being love*. Nowadays, the meaning of love has drastically drifted away from its scriptural semantics. For example, today, love is even associated with selfishness. However, the Apostle Paul defines love as follows: "Love worketh no ill to his neighbour: therefore love is the fulfilling of the law." (Romans 13:10) God is love, and therefore, he wants to save us by grace through faith in Jesus Christ.

Love is the essence that will abide. "And we have known and believed the love that God has for us. God is love, and he who abides in love abides in God, and God in him." (1 John 4:16) You abide in God by abiding in love. It is the glue that holds together both God and mankind. Furthermore, you will also abide in God if you confess that Jesus is the Son of God: "Whoever confesses that Jesus is the Son of God, God abides in him, and he in God." (1 John 4:15)

Love and fear do not match at all. Someone who claims to be born of the Spirit but manifests fear has surely not received Jesus. "There is no fear in love; but perfect love casts out fear, because fear involves torment. But he who fears has not been made perfect in love." (1 John 4:18) Through the transforming power of the holy Spirit, a person could be made perfect in love. Note, it is in passive voice!

You cannot accomplish perfection in love by *yourself*, but you need to allow *God*, who *is* love, to make you perfect in love. Fear will immediately disappear in your life once you realize the love of God and put your full trust in him.

Hence, love is an essential part of the teachings of our Lord and Savior Jesus Christ. "And Jesus answered him, The first of all the commandments *is*, Hear, O Israel; The Lord our God is one Lord: And thou shalt love the Lord thy God with all thy heart, and with all thy soul, and with all thy mind, and with all thy strength: this *is* the first commandment. And the second *is* like, *namely* this, Thou shalt love thy neighbour as thyself. There is none other commandment greater than these." (Mark 12:29-31) There is no greater commandment than to love God with all your heart, and to love your neighbor as yourself.

God's attributes: being eternal

God is *eternal*. It is he "who alone has immortality" (1 Timothy 6:16) Jesus is one with the Father, and he that sees Jesus sees the Father. Therefore, all attributes that Jesus has revealed about himself to us apply also to the Father. Jesus does not change. "Jesus Christ the same yesterday, and to day, and for ever." (Hebrews 13:8) Hence, God the Father does not change for all eternity. Being eternal means being eternal forever.

God's attributes: goodness

A further attribute of God is his *goodness*. "Good and upright is the LORD: therefore will he teach sinners in the way." (Psalms 25:8) A certain ruler approached Jesus and addressed him as "Good Master." (Luke 18:18) Listen to Jesus' response: "And Jesus said unto him, 'Why callest thou me good? none is good, save one, that is, God.' " (Luke 18:19) Jesus is very precise: nobody is good, except God.

However, God's goodness may be a problem for us, because he is good, and we are not! If we are not good, then we are evil. Evil in this context means that you do not have a relationship with Jesus, and thus are not a partaker of the divine nature that follows as a consequence of spiritual regeneration. In fact, without having received Christ we are still sinners and under sin's bondage: "For all have sinned, and come short of the glory of God." (Romans 3:23) And we know that the wages of sin is death. Sin will not exist forever. If you do not get rid of sin, you will not live forever!

It is said: "A good man out of the good treasure of the heart bringeth forth good things: and an evil man out of the evil treasure bringeth forth evil things." (Matthew 12:35) Obviously, it is possible to be a good person and also to bring about good things. How can this be accomplished? This is only possible if we have a good treasure within us. Only in Christ are we a new creature, having put on the clothes of Christ's righteousness. It is after the spiritual regeneration that we *are* good in Christ. Even our good works are a consequence of receiving Christ through faith. "For we are his workmanship, created in Christ Jesus unto good works, which God hath before ordained that we should walk in them." (Ephesians 2:10) God has ordained those good works, and we will walk in them once we are a new creation in Jesus Christ. Therefore, the key to continuing to exist before a good God is to *become* good "through the redemption that is in Christ Jesus." (Romans 3:24)

> A born-again person wants to do God's will, not in order to become holy, but because of *being* holy already.

God's attributes: holiness

God is *holy*. In general, holy means to be different, either in the sense of being different from the world or set apart. By default, we are not holy in the sense of how God is holy.

However, after being born of the Spirit and having received Christ into our lives, the Apostle Peter clearly points out to those who are in Christ as to be holy: "But ye are a chosen generation, a royal priesthood, an holy nation, a peculiar people; that ye should shew forth the praises of him who hath called you out of darkness into his marvellous light." (1 Peter 2:9) Those who have received Jesus, and thus have personally experienced the spiritual regeneration, are a *holy* nation.

What are we in Christ? We *are* holy. God is holy, and "as he which hath called you is holy, so be ye holy in all manner of conversation." (1 Peter 1:15) In our own strength we will fail to be holy simply because it is not possible to be holy by ourselves. To be holy means to belong to Christ. Only when we belong to Christ are we holy. Thus, in Christ we are holy as God is holy. No scriptural evidence is found that there are different kinds or levels of holiness. We are holy or we are not holy. There is no in-between!

What is the manifestation of holiness? It is the very fact that a holy person seeks to live in accordance with God's will in all his or her ways—not to *become* holy, but because they are already holy in Christ! You cannot be holy by your actions or any means of work. You need *to be made holy* by being "transformed by the renewing of your mind, that ye may prove what is that good, and acceptable, and perfect, will of God." (Romans 12:2) It is passive voice! It is by God's grace that we are made holy, "not by works of righteousness which we have done, but according to his mercy he saved us, by the washing of regeneration, and renewing of the Holy Ghost." (Titus 3:5) This is good news! This is the wonderful and assuring promise of God: he will transform you by the washing of regeneration and renewing of the holy Spirit and save you according to his mercy. God is holy. He does not only *want* you to be holy, but God also did everything to *make* you holy by receiving Jesus Christ into your heart.

God's attributes: being faithful

God is absolutely *faithful*. You can rely on him, always. The assurance of God to be faithful means that you really can trust in God. Whatever may happen in your life, trust in God, as he is faithful. God assures you that "all things work together for good to them that love God, to them who are the called according to his purpose." (Romans 8:28) If you are in Christ, you can trust in God's word that he works for the good in *all* things for those who love him. The Apostle Paul feels confident proclaiming a message of assurance: "If God is for us, who can be against us?" (Romans 8:31)

God's attributes: being merciful

Moreover, the heavenly Father is *merciful*. He freely offers eternal life in Jesus Christ. It is his very nature to love his creation. He does not want us to receive the wages of sin, that is death. Bear in mind that God's intentions toward us are perfectly summarized by the inspired words of the Apostle Paul: "God commendeth his love toward us, in that, while we were yet sinners, Christ died for us." (Romans 5:8)

What did *we* do to move God to love us? Nothing! On the contrary, we were sinners, we mistrusted the word of God and God himself, and thus, sin separated us from God. But what did *God* do? He sent his Son, Jesus Christ, to die for you and for me, even though we were still sinners. This is unconditional love and devotion. This is reason enough to proclaim: Great is our God!

> There is joy in the presence of the Lord Jesus. You do not want to miss it!

Paul continues: "Much more then, being now justified by his blood, we shall be saved from wrath through him." (Romans 5:9) By the blood of Jesus Christ we are justified and saved from the wages of sin, because we have received Christ through faith and experienced the spiritual regeneration. "For if, when we were enemies, we were reconciled to God by the death of his Son, much more, being reconciled, we shall be saved by *his* life." (Romans 5:10) Paul is saying that we were reconciled to God by the death of Jesus even as we were in enmity with God due to sin and our sinful nature.

> Even sin did not stop God's mercy toward his creation. Through Jesus' death and resurrection God proved his love for all eternity.

Jesus brings about reconciliation with God for *us*. We shall be saved because we have been reconciled to God, *not* by our effort and deeds, but by the death of Christ. Notice, Jesus reconciled us while we were yet enemies. "And not only that, but we also rejoice in God through our Lord Jesus Christ, through whom we have now received the reconciliation." (Romans 5:11) There is joy in the presence of the Lord who reconciled us to God. The Lord loved you even when you were still a sinner, and thus an enemy of God. How much more assured can you be of God's love toward you after you became a child of God through faith? Jesus says that he will by no means cast out someone who has come to him through faith!

God's attributes: being righteous

God is *righteous*. "The LORD is righteous in all his ways and faithful in all he does." (Psalms 145:17) There is no doubt about the righteousness of God. And what about

> Stop trying to make yourself righteous by means of what you do. It does not work!

you? Ask yourself the question: am I righteous? The answer to this question determines your eternal destiny. Why? Because unless you are righteous, you will not be saved: "and if the righteous scarcely be saved, where shall the ungodly and the sinner appear?" (1 Peter 4:18) The one who is unrighteous belongs to the group of sinners and ungodly people.

The impact of sin and its consequences is clearly defined. Remember that "the wages of sin is death." (Romans 6:23) Hence, if you are not righteous, you will surely die. There is no question about it. So if you do not want to die, you may want to start thinking about how you receive righteousness that keeps you alive in the presence of the Lord. You cannot make yourself righteous, due to the fact that you are not able to change your sinful nature by yourself. Stop trying! It is doomed to fail in the beginning. The Apostle Paul informs the saints in Rome with the following, most unambiguous, statements concerning the topic of being righteous: "For as by one man's disobedience many were made sinners, so by the obedience of one shall many be made righteous." (Romans 5:19) In the first part of the statement, Paul is talking about Adam, the first human being, who lost his divine and eternal nature by disobedience toward God. Thus, sin entered into this world and its manifestations started to run rampant. Because of Adam's mistrust toward God, many people were made sinners.

On the contrary, the obedience of Jesus will make many righteous. Wait a moment. What will make you righteous? It is the obedience of *Jesus*, not your own! If you are in Christ you are righteous, because you become a partaker of his righteousness through faith: "Therefore being justified by faith, we have peace with God through our Lord Jesus Christ." (Romans 5:1) What a wonderful message!

> Salvation is found in Jesus Christ – exclusively.

God's attributes: peace with God

You are justified by faith in Jesus Christ, and as a consequence, it is promised to have peace with God! And yet, if you do not have peace with God, then examine yourself and your standing with Him. You have enough reason to be glad and to rejoice in the Lord! You transcend from death to life in and through Christ. This is a strong affirmation of assurance of salvation. Assurance of salvation is not a farce at all. God is love, eternal, good, holy, faithful, merciful, and righteous. God's attributes are incredible and nearly too good to be true. But they *are* true!

Jesus, the way to salvation

"For God sent not his Son into the world to condemn the world; but that the world through him might be saved." (John3:17) God's intention is to save you from the consequences of sin. He offers you salvation in Christ. "Neither is there salvation in any other: for there is none other name under heaven given among men, whereby we must be saved." (Acts 4:12) The *only* way to God is through Jesus and to believe in him. It is not your potential church membership, your high intellect, your talents, or generous donations that will prepare and make you ready for the final day of judgment at Christ's return. Paul makes it clear: "For I am not ashamed of the gospel of Christ: for it is the power of God unto salvation to every one that believeth; to the Jew first, and also to the Greek." (Romans 1:16) It is the Gospel of Christ that has the power to transform your life and sinful nature.

There is no power except in the blood of Jesus, which is able to transform someone's nature from being sinful to being righteous and divine. It is by no means any pastor, evangelist, church, religious system, or the like. It is through Jesus Christ alone!

Salvation—ready to be picked up

Salvation is not based upon you and your performance. It is something that can be received through faith, because it is already there! This is important to understand: salvation is something that has already been prepared by God through Jesus Christ. The gift of eternal life is ready to be picked up. Its reality and existence do not depend on you. Thus, whether you believe it or not, it does not make any difference in its

> Faith is the only means to pick up the free gift of salvation.

presence; salvation has already been provided for all mankind, because "God so loved the world." (John 3:16) The Apostle John declares the truth about Jesus: "And he is the propitiation for our sins: and not for ours only, but also for the sins of the whole world." (1 John 2:2) Jesus successfully dealt with our sins.

The price has been paid, so to say, by Jesus. "For even the Son of man came not to be ministered unto, but to minister, and to give his life a ransom for many." (Mark 10:45) In Christ we are children of God and "if children, then heirs; heirs of God, and joint-heirs with Christ." (Romans 8:17) Isn't that wonderful and liberating? Salvation has been fully accomplished through Christ. You do not need to add anything to the accomplished work of Christ. In fact, you are not even able to do so. Thus, why do you try to do so?

Salvation, will you pick it up?

Salvation is independent of anyone's actions, but it is the result of God's love toward you. But, of course, it *does* make a difference whether you pick it up or not. It is like being at a table in a restaurant, where all kinds of delicacies are offered. The delicacies are there, whether you sit at table or not. You can observe the food, analyze, and even philosophize over it. But unless you taste it, you will not get satisfied. You literally need to receive the food to stop being hungry. Likewise, you can talk about salvation in Christ and do this or that. But it does not literally save you. You need to pick up salvation that is in Christ. The means to pick up salvation is *faith*. Through faith you receive Jesus and its gift of eternal life.

Salvation cannot be earned by yourself, but it has already been provided by God through Jesus Christ. Faith is the means to *receive* the gift of salvation. Thus, you can and will have assurance of salvation once you have received salvation through faith. Remember, salvation is something that *God* has already provided for you and me, and it has nothing to do with your own performance. Salvation in Christ is merely a matter of whether you pick it up or not. God wants all mankind to be saved, but he is not pushy. He offers salvation, but he lets *you* decide whether to pick it up or not. God does not violate your free will, neither is it his intention for you to be a mere puppet in his hand. It is about time to make a decision to either accept the gift of salvation in Christ or reject it. It is up to you!

Salvation, a necessity for a fallen mankind

Why is there a need for salvation for mankind? We heard that after Adam's mistrust of God's word, and hence God himself, sin entered the world. In the beginning, however, God created the world and said that his creation was very good. Everything was in perfect harmony with each other.

Things changed immediately after mistrust of God's word set in. Sin entered the world, and with it, all its evil manifestations, like murder, fear, mistrust, feelings of forsakenness, jealousy, low self-esteem, hatred, and unfortunately, much more. All descendants of Adam were born into a sinful world and with a sinful nature. Salvation from this sinful nature is necessary for mankind to not be condemned, but to have eternal life. The wages of sin is death—the universal law of non-divine nature.

Let us have a closer look at what the sinful nature of

fallen mankind means. You may remember the occurrence of the discussion between a Pharisee and Jesus concerning the topic of salvation: "Jesus answered, 'Verily, verily, I say unto thee, Except a man be born of water and of the Spirit, he cannot enter into the kingdom of God. That which is born of the flesh is flesh; and that which is born of the Spirit is spirit. Marvel not that I said unto thee, Ye must be born again.' " (John 3:5-7) What Jesus says here is basically that, by default, you are born of the flesh, which is the sinful nature, so to say. Therefore, you do mind the things of the flesh." (Romans 8:5)

The consequences of being born of the flesh are fatal, as Paul says: "For to be carnally minded is death; but to be spiritually minded is life and peace. Because the carnal mind is enmity against God: for it is not subject to the law of God, neither indeed can be. So then they that are in the flesh cannot please God." (Romans 8:6-8) This text dramatically tells you the consequence of being of the flesh, or in other words, to be carnally minded—it is death. And death itself is the wages of sin. Thus, the circle is closing. But the good news is that there is a way out of being carnally minded. You need to be born again. You need to have an encounter with Jesus Christ!

Salvation—becoming a new creation

The only way out of the dilemma of sin is to be born of water and of the Spirit. It means to be born into a spiritual dimension, and so to be transformed from being carnally minded to being spiritually minded. The consequence of being born again is to be free from sin, as it was before sin entered the world. In order to experience the transformation in nature, from carnal to spiritual, Jesus needs to be received as Savior and Lord. In Christ you are "a new creature: old things are passed away; behold, all things are become new." (2 Corinthians 5:17) It is a new birth in a spiritual sense.

How do you get rid of your sinful nature? It is by receiving Christ in whom you are a new creature—you are born of the Spirit. "But ye are not in the flesh, but in the Spirit, if so be that the Spirit of God dwell in you. Now if any man have not the Spirit of Christ, he is none of his." (Romans 8:9) When do you know to be in the Spirit? It is when the Spirit of God dwells in you. If the holy Spirit does not dwell in you, it is clear evidence that you have not been born again.

How can you be sure that you have the holy Spirit? You will have the Spirit if you ask the heavenly Father to give you the holy Spirit: "If ye then, being evil, know how to give good gifts unto your children: how much more shall your heavenly Father give the Holy Spirit to them that ask him?" (Luke 11:13) God does not lie, and he is faithful. Simply ask, and it will be given unto you. God is trustworthy! To be in Christ automatically demonstrates one to be on the safe side, or rather, *saved* side. You are a partaker of the divine nature, a child of God, and hence heirs of Jesus and his promise of eternal life, which is guaranteed by Jesus and his work of atonement already accomplished for the sins of the world.

> In Christ you are not only on the safe side, but on the saved side!

The atoning work of Jesus Christ

Christ is *the* key element within God's plan of salvation. Why is Jesus the key element in the context of salvation? The answer is very simple, namely John 3:16: "For God so loved the world, that he gave his only begotten Son, that whosoever believeth in him should not perish, but have everlasting life." To believe in Christ means to be a designated heir of eternal life.

Furthermore, what does it mean that God *gave* his Son Jesus Christ? The answer to this question is quite obvious: in Jesus Christ, God offered us life. God did it, because he continuously loves us. "He that spared not his own Son, but delivered him up for us all, how shall he not with him also freely give us all things?" (Romans 8:32) God freely gives us all things, because Jesus accomplished the work of redemption.

> Jesus Christ laid down his life for you, so that you may live!

What did Jesus *actually* do to make salvation possible? To answer this question, let us have a look at two inspired statements. First, John says: "Hereby perceive we the love of God, because he laid down his life for us." (1 John 3:16) Second, Paul mentions an essential detail: "Who gave himself for our sins, that he might deliver us from this present evil world, according to the will of God and our Father." (Galatians 1:4) Jesus died for *us*! He died for the sins of the world with a specific purpose, namely to deliver fallen mankind from this evil world.

Paul summarizes the work of Jesus as follows: "For I delivered unto you first of all that which I also received, how that Christ died for our sins according to the scriptures; and that he was buried, and that he rose again the third day according to the scriptures." (1 Corinthians 15:3-5) In his letter to the Romans Paul gets to the heart of the issue and testifies of Jesus: "Who was delivered for our offences, and was raised again for our justification." (Romans 4:25) Jesus died for you and for me. And if you believe in him, you *will* have eternal life. It is assured.

Jesus Christ, the resurrection and the life

Jesus once said to Martha, the sister of Lazarus: "I am the resurrection, and the life: he that believeth in me, though he were dead, yet shall he live." (John 11:25) Everyone who believes in Jesus will live. Notice what John assures you: "I write unto you, little children, because your sins are forgiven you for his name's sake." (1 John 2:12) Your sins are forgiven! In Christ you are set free from the bondage of sin, because Jesus eliminated the power of sin by condemning sin in *his* flesh. You have nothing to fear as long as you stay in the presence of the Lord and Savior Jesus Christ. He paid the price of sin with his precious life to save a fallen mankind!

As in the times of Noah, people do not want to trust in God's word— even at the cost of their lives.

Through Adam sin entered the world. "Wherefore, as by one man sin entered into the world, and death by sin; and so death passed upon all men, for that all have sinned." (Romans 5:12) Sin separates from a holy God, but God did not turn away from his creation. He still loves his creation! However, he *does* hate sin. Therefore, God provided a way out of this sin's dilemma through Jesus Christ.

Listen to what Paul emphasizes in his following statement: "Therefore as by the offence of one judgment came upon all men to condemnation; even so by the righteousness of one the free gift came upon all men unto justification of life. For as by one man's disobedience many were made sinners, so by the obedience of one shall many be made righteous." (Romans 5:18, 19) Due to the obedience of Jesus, you now have the possibility to choose between death and life, respectively.

Unfortunately, not everyone wants to listen to Jesus and his wonderful message. Jesus preached about heavenly matters and taught the truth. At that time many followers of Jesus turned their backs on him, because they wanted to listen to those teachers who were teaching what they actually wanted to hear, *even* at the cost of their lives. Paul warned his dearly beloved son Timothy against such a wrong attitude: "For the time will come when they will not endure sound doctrine; but after their own lusts shall they heap to themselves teachers, having itching ears; and they shall turn away their ears from the truth, and shall be turned unto fables." (2 Timothy 4:3, 4)

Jesus openly asked his twelve disciples, "Will ye also go away?" (John 6:67) Jesus asks *you* personally if you want to approach him or go away. It is your choice! "Simon Peter answered him, 'Lord, to whom shall we go? thou hast the words of eternal life. And we believe and are sure that thou art that Christ, the Son of the living God.' " (John 6:68, 69) Simon Peter was sure about the fact that Jesus is *the* life. What about you?

Are you sure that Jesus is the life, the Son of the living God, and the Savior of the world? Have you already had a personal encounter with the Lord who died for your sins? Have you received Christ in your life? Have you been set free? It is about time to examine yourself! If you are not able to answer those questions, or you feel unsure how to answer them, it might be an indicator that you have not yet experienced true freedom, peace, and joy in Christ. In this context, remember the illustration of the apple: if you have experienced a fresh and tasty apple by literally eating it, you know what it tastes like. If someone asked you later whether

> Have you received Christ in your life? Take sides!

you know the apple's taste or not, you can immediately respond without any hesitation. Your answer would instantaneously be a resounding *yes*. Now, face the truth: What is your relationship to Christ? Do you know *about* him, or do you really know *him*?

Take sides, today!

"To day if ye will hear his voice, harden not your hearts." (Hebrews 3:15) It is about time to decide whom to serve! It is about time to receive Christ! It is about time to grab the gift of God that is eternal life in Christ Jesus! It is about time to believe and accept salvation that has already been worked out for your sake through Jesus Christ.

The very moment of the second coming of Christ changes everything. In particular, it terminates the time of grace to repent and the possibility to take sides. However, there are two additional scenarios that are essential and may terminate the time of grace to turn to God: blasphemy against the holy Spirit (Matthew 12:22-33) and, of course, the time of your own death.

Blasphemy against the holy Spirit

Blasphemy against the holy Spirit means that you consciously ridicule the work of the holy Spirit in the lives of men and even ascribe it to the devil. This is exactly what the Pharisees did concerning the works and miracles Jesus accomplished through the power of the holy Spirit. They well knew that these things could only be possible by God's Spirit. But they classified Christ's work to be of the devil. If you attribute the work of the holy Spirit to the devil, you are not able to approach God. Why? Because you are mocking the very holy Spirit who is the one leading you to repentance. "My little children, these things write I unto you, that ye sin not. And if any man sin, we have an advocate with the Father, Jesus Christ the righteous." (1 John 2:1) Having been born again into the body of Christ, it is not your nature and will anymore to constantly *remain* in sin. You feel the urge to live in harmony with your new creature's want, which is indeed focused on holy things. However, if you fall back into your previous sinful habits, the holy Spirit who dwells in you confidently leads you to the feet of Jesus. It is there that you find peace and true repentance of your rebellion against God.

> Never get into a discussion with Satan. You will surely lose!

Death and its reality

The time of death may also terminate the time of grace to repent. You do not know when this moment of death may knock at your door. Basically, the Psalmist David draws attention to the reality of death for everyone: "So teach us to number our days, that we may apply our hearts unto wisdom." (Psalms 90:12)

Most people live as though there will always be a tomorrow. They live their lives as though they will never die.

Satan himself is the originator of that lie. It is an evil deception that distracts mankind from their destiny. At the time of Adam and Eve, look how Satan deceived them, and which lie he used to attack them on a spiritual level. First, he sowed a small but effective portion of doubt: "And he said unto the woman, 'Yea, hath God said, Ye shall not eat of every tree of the garden?' " (Genesis 3:1) Satan questioned the words of God. He sowed mistrust for God in Eve, and even planted the idea that there is at least the possibility that God could have potentially lied to them. What happened next? Eve started a fatal discussion with the father of the lie. (John 8:44) Satan was subtle in his argumentation. As it turned out later, Eve made the wrong decision to listen to and discuss God's words with Satan. Don't argue with Satan. You will surely lose!

God obviously instructed Eve of the deadly consequences of eating the fruit. Eve told Satan that God had not allowed her to eat from the fruit, lest she will die. Satan immediately struck back: "Ye shall not surely die." (Genesis 3:4) This is the great lie that made mankind fall: Eve and Adam *did* eat the fruit, sin entered the world, and death started to reign. This is the lie that will be one of the main reasons the majority of today's mankind will die in its sins. This lie is constantly proclaiming: "Ye shall not surely die." (Genesis 3:4)

The truth is found in the words of our Creator: "And as it is appointed unto men once to die, but after this the judgment: so Christ was once offered to bear the sins of many; and unto them that look for him shall he appear the second time without sin unto salvation." (Hebrews 9:27, 28) This verse contains a very powerful message. As a matter of

<table><tr><td>

Live in the Spirit – a strong set of cards!

</td><td>

fact, it summarizes the Gospel of Jesus Christ. First of all, you and I will die at some point. This is determined and truly beyond question, unless Jesus returns first! However, death is not the end of the story.

</td></tr></table>

After you have died, you come into the final judgment. Jesus knows that nobody can literally survive the righteous judgment of God. Therefore, Jesus was offered to bear the sins of the world. Everyone who receives Jesus as his or her personal Savior and Lord will be saved. For those who are in Christ Jesus will appear the second time to bring incorruption and immortality.

Satan does not want you to know the truth. Why? Because the truth sets you free and provides peace of mind. It eradicates all evil manifestations of uncertainty in your life. Your spiritual blinkers will be taken off from your eyes so that you can see clearly. You are kind of entering into the spiritual world and experiencing its reality! Take the plunge!

Watch and pray!

In a nutshell: There are three essential scenarios that may terminate your personal time of grace and your freedom to take sides. They are Christ's return, your time of death, and speaking against the holy Spirit. Let us always be ready and prepared for all of those scenarios. We do not know which one applies in our lives! Jesus advises the sincere seeker of truth, "Watch ye and pray, lest ye enter into temptation. The spirit truly is ready, but the flesh is weak." (Mark 14:38)

It is about time to grab eternal life, which is only found in Christ through faith. Seek the presence of the Lord and remember the gift of God: it is eternal life in Christ! God assures you: "See, I have set before thee this day life and good, and death and evil." (Deuteronomy 30:15) What do you choose? Furthermore, he says: "For the wages of sin is death; but the gift of God is eternal life through Jesus Christ our Lord." (Romans 6:23) You can rely on Jesus and his merits, and therefore "also joy in God through our Lord Jesus Christ, by whom we have now received the atonement." (Romans 5:11) You do not need to fear death at all. Jesus is the life, and you become a partaker of his life by receiving Christ through faith. Receiving Christ is not necessarily accompanied by feelings or similar. It simply means to receive the gift of salvation through faith. By receiving Christ the holy Spirit dwells in you and lets the fruit of the Spirit spring out of your heart.

Whom do *you* trust? On which side are *you* putting yourself? On the bright side of life, or on the dark side of death? Consciously decide which side you want to be on. The choice is yours!

Do not grieve the holy Spirit

The holy Spirit shows you negative and captivating things in your life that God wants to eliminate to enable you to grow spiritually. Aside from you, God also knows the lifestyle you are manifesting in your life. Stop playing the game of deceiving yourself, others, and, first and foremost, God! Do not grieve the holy Spirit. Honestly try to enter into a dialog with yourself and find out what priorities are on your life's agenda.

Once you have found the answer to what you really believe and which values actually dominate your life, start reconsidering your life's focus and spiritual orientation. Do you love God? Do you have a personal relationship with God in Christ? Your answer may be yes, but you might find out that you do not really love God with all your heart, nor have a relationship with him at all. In that case, I want to encourage you to get on your knees right now and ask Jesus to come into your heart. Ask the heavenly Father to give you the holy Spirit, who will truly open your eyes. Thus, do not grieve the holy Spirit in case he shows you your sinful habits within your life. You will truly get to know your spiritual standing if you let the holy Spirit work in you. Why? Because the holy Spirit will guide you into all truth, which sets you free, indeed.

Even when you do not feel anything

There might be times in your spiritual life's journey where you become truly worried about, or even afraid of having lost your salvation and eternal life. Let the following words be words of encouragement and comfort. Being in Christ means to be a child of God. Being a child of God means to be an heir of the things to come. Jesus will never cast you out of his family. Remember, you are saved because you received Christ, and his atoning work of redemption! You might think that you have done too many evil things in your life. God hates sin, yes, this is absolutely true. But the truth is, God loves *you*!

> Do not look at you missing out. Look unto Jesus!

In Christ sin and its manifestations are not a problem anymore, because, once and for all, they have been dealt with *already*: on the cross at Calvary, where the Savior of the world died for sinners and cried out: 'it is finished!' If you confess your sins, believe it, in Christ they are washed away. You do not need to feel anything! Your salvation in Christ is absolutely not dependent on what you feel or what you do not feel. Do not look at you missing out, but look unto Jesus and his victory over sin and death!

Ask yourself the crucial question: Do I have the desire to repent and turn to God anew? Do I feel sorry for doing things that are in direct contrast to the will of God? If yes, let me tell you something, the holy Spirit is working in you! It is the holy Spirit who leads you to repentance! Paul once said: "Or despisest thou the riches of his goodness and forbearance and longsuffering; not knowing that the goodness of God leadeth thee to repentance?" (Romans 2:4)

In fact, God's goodness leads you to repentance. What is the goodness of God? It is an aspect of the fruit of the Spirit. "But the fruit of the Spirit is love, joy, peace, longsuffering, gentleness, goodness, faith, meekness, temperance." (Galatians 5:22) Goodness originates from God himself and is a manifestation of the holy Spirit in you. Without the holy Spirit, who would have led you to repentance?

It is not you who seeks repentance, but the holy Spirit *in* you calls your attention to repent. Finally, repentance leads to salvation. "For godly sorrow worketh repentance to salvation not to be repented of: but the sorrow of the world worketh death." (2 Corinthians 7:10) Therefore, put your trust in God's word of assurance, and do not focus on your own feelings!

One day the heavenly books are opened

"And I saw the dead, small and great, stand before God; and the books were opened: and another book was opened, which is the book of life: and the dead were judged out of those things which were written in the books, according to their works." (Revelation 20:12) Although you might have in mind this judgment scene with negative connotations, you do not need to be fearful. "There is no fear in love." (1 John 4:18) In the name of Jesus you can be confident even when you stand before God's judgment seat. Why? "There is therefore now no condemnation to them which are in Christ Jesus, who walk not after the flesh, but after the Spirit." (Romans 8:1)

> In Christ you stand fearlessly in front of God's judgment seat for there is no condemnation in Christ.

In Christ you are righteous and will not be condemned. "He that believeth on him is not condemned: but he that believeth not is condemned already, because he hath not believed in the name of the only begotten Son of God." (John 3:18) Again, the key to eternal life is to believe in the Son of God!

The one who believes in Jesus "is passed from death unto life." (John 5:24) No fear, no uncertainty, no doubt, but assurance of salvation in Jesus Christ. "Let us therefore come boldly unto the throne of grace, that we may obtain mercy, and find grace to help in time of need." (Hebrews 4:16) You will find grace galore in the presence of the Lord!

Let your sins be washed away

Let me tell you the truth: if you do not feel worthy of approaching God's presence and his throne of grace because of your sins and misbehavior, but you truly have the urge to repent, *then* you are worthy all the more! Come to Jesus and surrender your life unto him who has already died for your sins, for all your weaknesses, and for your inability to change and literally get rid of your sinful nature.

Jesus will completely wash away your sinful nature and transform it into a divine nature which is perfect in Christ. "For by one offering he hath perfected for ever them that are sanctified." (Hebrews 10:14) This is the truth: There is only one sacrifice that suffices to free you from the bondage of sin and your sinful nature. If you have not yet experienced its reality, turn to God, who will send you the holy Spirit to guide you into all truth!

Some people may say that God is only a prayer away. But the truth is that even *before* you pray or approach God, he is already there. You do not need to soften or appease him in any respect. In fact, God is already waiting for you to approach him. Do not forget the godly promise: through the holy Spirit, he is "nigh unto all them that call upon him, to all that call upon him in truth." (Psalms 145:18)

Live a happy life as God's heir in Christ!

The assurance of salvation in Christ is essential to live a happy and confident spiritual life. It takes away life's pressure to please God in any conceivable way in order to receive eternal life in return. You cannot earn anything through whatever comes into your mind!

Grace does not mean to do something in order to get something, but to receive forgiveness of sins and salvation from a merciful God! You were not redeemed with corruptible things, for example, by your works or deeds of any kind, "but with the precious blood of Christ, as of a lamb without blemish and without spot." (1 Peter 1:19) There are further unambiguous statements underlining the cleansing power of the blood of Jesus. For example, through grace God "hath made us accepted in the beloved. In whom we have redemption through his blood, the forgiveness of sins, according to the riches of his grace." (Ephesians 1:6, 7) And

> An heir receives what is to be inherited. By definition.

"If the Son therefore shall make you free, ye shall be free indeed." (John 8:36) These are inspired testimonies of Paul and John. It can also be your personal testimony!

In Christ you are a child of God. "But when the fulness of the time was come, God sent forth his Son, made of a woman, made under the law, to redeem them that were under the law, that we might receive the adoption of sons. And because ye are sons, God hath sent forth the Spirit of his Son into your hearts, crying, Abba, Father. Wherefore thou art no more a servant, but a son; and if a son, then an heir of God through Christ." (Galatians 4:4-7) According to Paul, Jesus came to this world that we may receive the adoption of sons and the holy Spirit into our hearts.

We are children of God, and therefore heirs of God through Christ. By definition, heirs receive their inheritance. Heirs do not have to do anything to receive something they inherited. Once you are an heir, you will without doubt receive the inheritance.

Now Paul tells us that we are heirs of God. Thus, we will receive the eternal inheritance, which is eternal life, once we received Christ into our lives. These are words of encouragement! Believe it! It is not an assurance based on what you did, but it is the assurance you shall have in Jesus through faith. "And this is the promise that he hath promised us, even eternal life." (1 John 2:25)

Jesus assures life that is in him

"He that hath the Son hath life; and he that hath not the Son of God hath not life." (1 John 5:12) John was absolutely convinced that a person in Christ is saved. In one of his letters, John even proclaims the following statement concerning assurance of salvation: "These things have I written unto you that believe on the name of the Son of God; that ye may know that ye have eternal life, and that ye may believe on the name of the Son of God." (1 John 5:13) There is no doubt about the fact that in Christ you have assurance of salvation. This is good news!

Let us meet at the pool of Siloam

Once there was a man who had been blind since his birth. He could not see anything. Jesus passed by, saw this man, and healed him completely by making a clay of his own spittle and putting it on the eyes of the blind man. Jesus told him to go and wash in the pool of Siloam. "So the man went and washed, and came home seeing." (John 9:7) Jesus healed the blind man, and now he could see. What a wonderful message!

There is a spiritual teaching in this occurrence of the blind man being healed. Let us examine its deeper meaning. The word Siloam means "sent." The blind man experienced first-hand what it means to be *sent* by Jesus. If you are sent by the Lord, Jesus opens your eyes *first* to be able to see clearly! Otherwise, it is not possible to be a messenger of Christ. "Can the blind lead the blind? Will they not both fall into a pit?" (Luke 6:39) First you need to *see* before you are able to teach and lead others to the source of truth, Jesus

Christ, the Son of man.

Let us meet at the pool of Siloam, spiritual reality

What do you need to see, or rather, what *will* you see after you have received Christ? It is the spiritual reality. You will know Jesus Christ as your personal Savior and Lord. You will freely participate in a learning process called sanctification. Your life will change. Your lifestyle will begin to transform, step by step. You will have the urge to tell others about Jesus, and you will have assurance of salvation that is found in Christ through faith by grace. These manifestations of faith are real.

If you cannot identify with those elements listed above, then I highly recommend you examine yourself and your relationship with God. Do you know God, or do you know *about* him? The answer to this question will help you to examine yourself and dig deeper into your inner core of what you really believe and aim for in life.

Briefly, you need to have a personal encounter with the Lord Jesus himself in order to really understand what truth is. And I assure you that once you have experienced it, at the latest, then you will definitely know what I am talking about, not only in theory, but in practice. There is no magic involved, but it is God's supernatural power working on and *in* you.

Let us meet at the pool of Siloam, the clay

Let us have a look at how the story with the healing of the blind man continued. Jesus sent the blind man to the pool to wash. After being washed, the man returned seeing! The blind man accepted the clay from Jesus to be put on his eyes. He trusted in Jesus' power to heal him, and he was healed! In Revelation John talks about the Laodiceans who believed that they saw clearly in a spiritual sense, but actually they were not. And they were not even aware of their situation. Anyway, one of the attributes of the Laodiceans is spiritual blindness. "And knowest not that thou art wretched, and miserable, and poor, and blind, and naked." (Revelation 3:17) Therefore, the Laodiceans are advised to "anoint thine eyes with eyesalve, that thou mayest see." (Revelation 3:18) The Laodiceans shall anoint their eyes with eye salve in order to see, likewise the blind man was told to use the clay and let it be put on his eyes. Both shall be healed by trusting in Jesus Christ.

You will never be disappointed by trusting Jesus. He is faithful!

In the spiritual sense, the clay represents the eye salve. Who opens our eyes so that we can see spiritually? It is the holy Spirit, of whom is said: "And when he is come, he will reprove the world of sin, and of righteousness, and of judgment: of sin, because they believe not on me; of righteousness, because I go to my Father, and ye see me no more; Of judgment, because the prince of this world is judged." (John 16:8) Moreover, it is the Spirit of God who "will guide you into all truth." (John 16:13) Thus, the clay and the eye salve both represent the holy Spirit.

Furthermore, the man even accepted Jesus' command to go to the pool and to wash. To do God's will is an act of trust. And that is exactly what the blind man did, put trust in Jesus' words to him. The result was that he was healed by the power of God.

Let us meet at the pool of Siloam, leading to Christ

There is another deep spiritual teaching in the story of the blind man washing in the pool of Siloam: why did Jesus not heal the blind man immediately after touching him? It surely would have been a breeze for Jesus. It is because this account provides us a very important spiritual teaching, that is the Gospel of Christ. The blind man was desperate and not able to help himself to get rid of his blindness. It literally was his nature to be blind. Then Jesus came into play and gave him *the means* to *becoming* healed. Symbolically, it was the clay that Jesus gave to the man. But in the spiritual sense, the clay represents no one else than the holy Spirit.

It is the holy Spirit who is the means for us to being led into all truth and to being able to spiritually see. The holy Spirit leads us to Christ and makes us able to receive the gift of salvation through faith by God's grace, which "hath made us accepted in the beloved." (Ephesians 1:6) It was Jesus *himself* who provided the clay, or eye salve in the meaning of the book of Revelation, for the blind man. Jesus himself gave it to the man, personally. After the blind man received the clay, he decided to do according to the command of Jesus: he went to the pool and washed away the clay and was healed as his eyes were opened to see clearly. The blind man heard the words of Jesus and acted accordingly. This is true also today! How will you respond to the gentle call of Jesus?

Let us meet at the pool of Siloam, accept or reject

What was the blind man doing with the gift Jesus had provided for him? In other words: what are *you* doing with the gift of receiving the holy Spirit who is offered by God through Jesus Christ? The blind man made use of it in the exact way Jesus told him to do. He went to the pool and washed away the clay on his eyes. It is not recorded anywhere that the blind man argued with Jesus about what had to be done for him to see. He simply trusted in the words of the Savior and followed him, even literally. The result? The blindness was gone! He experienced the transforming power of God. You can experience it in the same manner by receiving the holy Spirit.

> After an encounter with Jesus you will never be the same! You will be amazed what you have been missing so far!

Receive the holy Spirit from God, the Father, who gives the holy Spirit "to them that ask him" (Luke 11:13) and listen to and act according to what he tells you to do! It will have the same positive consequences as with the blind man. You will be able to *see*—your spiritual blindness will be gone. Have the guts to get in contact with your Savior and Lord Jesus Christ in prayer and literally face the truth! You will be amazed what you have been missing so far.

You will have similar reactions to the once-blind man had after his eyesight was restored. The man was overwhelmed by the fact that he could now see. His nature of being blind was literally transformed into a new creation that now could see! Likewise, you will be transformed from a nature of spiritual blindness to a nature of spiritual clear-sightedness.

Let us meet at the pool of Siloam, personal experience

After being asked by the Pharisees who had healed him, the man told them that it was Jesus. Basically, this man did not know a lot about Jesus. But he emphasized: "whether he be a sinner or no, I know not: one thing I know, that, whereas I was blind, now I see." (John 9:25) Knowledge is important, but kind of just nice to have.

However, knowing the truth is *essential!* The man did not know Jesus by mere hearsay, but by personal experience. This is what counts most at the end.

Now, what does this story of the healing of the blind man have to do with us? In the same way Jesus approached the blind man, he also does with you and me today. Accept Jesus' solution to sin's problem, that is his shed blood, and follow God's will "not of the letter, but of the spirit." (2 Corinthians 3:6).

Remember, you cannot truly serve God unless you have the Spirit of God living in you! The Apostle Paul is talking about the importance of the *washing of regeneration* that is the spiritual regeneration, being born of water and of the Spirit. By the spiritual regeneration, you become a new creature in Christ that is holy and just in the eyes of God. Believe it—it is true! Come to Jesus and receive him into your life. And you will never be the same! You will notice that your spiritual perception increases tremendously, and the spiritual realm will become reality in your everyday life. The formerly blind man's exclamation will become your personal spiritual experience: "I was blind, but now I see."

Assurance of salvation, found in Jesus alone

Assurance of salvation is found only in Christ. "Neither is there salvation in any other: for there is none other name under heaven given among men, whereby we must be saved." (Acts 4:12) It is in the name of Jesus that you shall be saved. Jesus is *the* Savior and Lord who offers eternal life to everyone. Only those who believe in the Son of God and personally receive him will be partakers of the eternal inheritance.

Assurance of salvation, enduring the cross

By faith in the redeeming blood of Christ you have been justified. Therefore, you have peace with God through the Lord Jesus Christ, who is "the author and finisher of our faith; who for the joy that was set before him endured the cross, despising the shame, and is set down at the right hand of the throne of God." (Hebrews 12:2)

> Jesus endured the cross to save you and me.

Incidentally, the second part of this verse answers the question of why Jesus actually endured the cross. He died for you, for the joy that was set before him. The joy of Jesus was to save mankind from the bondage of sin. He wants to save as many people as possible. The motivation and mission of Jesus was "to seek and to save that which was lost." (Luke 19:10)

Even in the parable of the lost sheep, Jesus points out his love for mankind. "What man of you, having an hundred sheep, if he lose one of them, doth not leave the ninety and nine in the wilderness, and go after that which is lost, until he find it?" (Luke 15:4) Jesus goes after that which is lost. He does it for you as if you were the only person in this world. And he looks for you until he finds you. What a wonderful message! What a great and loving God we have! Will you invite Jesus in?

Assurance of salvation, the author and finisher

Now let us turn to the first part of Hebrews 12:2. It is Jesus who is the author, and even beginning of your faith. Likewise, Jesus is the finisher of your faith. Saving faith is a gift of God and not your achievement at all. "For by grace are ye saved through faith; and that not of yourselves: it is the gift of God: not of works, lest any man should boast." (Ephesians 2:8, 9)

> Faith is not a result of your personal endeavor, but a gift of God.

Moreover, "faith cometh by hearing, and hearing by the word of God." (Romans 10:17) Faith is not a result or consequence of your personal endeavor, but it comes by hearing. By hearing what? Faith comes by hearing God's word.

Dear reader, do you really have peace with God? Is it pure theory so far? Unless you have peace of mind in Christ, examine yourself *whether* you are in Christ or not! Even if you have been a follower of Christ for a long time already, come to Jesus and invite him in anew in case you do not have peace with God and true affirmation of having eternal life in Christ. Ask God the Father to give you the holy Spirit, and believe that you have already received him in the very moment you ask for him. God wants you to be sure about having eternal life in Christ!

Assurance of salvation, to feel or not to feel

Assurance of salvation is an invariant, an unchangeable givenness. It has *nothing* to do with feelings. On the contrary, whether you kind of feel saved in Christ or not, it does not change the very fact that you *are* saved in Christ. Your state of salvation is completely independent of your feelings. In many cases, feelings may influence our perception and discernment tremendously. When it comes to spiritual discernment, feelings are not to be trusted nor are they the basis to rely on. Feelings come and go. They are both passing impressions and expressions in one's life.

However, the holy Spirit testifies with our spirit that we are children of God. It is him who teaches you and guides you into all truth. It is the holy Spirit who gives real discernment of spirits, so that you know what is right and what is wrong. Who will provide you with wisdom about what is truth and what is not truth? It is the holy Spirit. You do not need to rely on unstable feelings. The holy Spirit will constantly guide you on your spiritual journey.

> The sacrifice of Christ is sufficient. You are already a winner in Christ.

Assurance of salvation, John 3:16

Assurance of salvation is by no means a mere feeling, but the very reality in Christ. Assurance of salvation is exclusively found in Christ through faith. *In Christ*, because Jesus died on the cross for us all, so that we may live by receiving him; *through faith* we have access to the gift of forgiveness of sins and all of our iniquity; *by grace* we are saved, not because of our works, but because God loves us and wants us to be saved and rescued from the day of wrath.

God sent his Son Jesus Christ that whosoever believes in him will not be condemned, but has eternal life. This is what John 3:16 is all about: *it is about having faith in Christ unto salvation.* Christ is enough. His sacrifice is enough. You do not need to add anything. It is not even possible to add something at all. Jesus himself cried out for the sake of you and me: "It is finished." (John 19:30)

There is no place for feelings of uncertainty when it comes to assurance of salvation in Christ for those who are born of water and of the Spirit and have experienced the washing of regeneration "not of the letter, but of the spirit." (2 Corinthians 3:6) There is no doubt about it. Death has been defeated. "Where, O death, is your victory? Where, O death, is your sting? The sting of death is sin, and the power of sin is the law. But thanks be to God! He gives us the victory through our Lord Jesus Christ. Therefore, my dear brothers and sisters, stand firm. Let nothing move you." (1 Corinthians 15:55-58) What a wonderful and profound message of assurance and delight! God gives us victory through Jesus! Period. Our part is to stand firm and not to be moved by anything!

Religion and other dangers

Satan does not like the message of hope of eternal life which is in Christ. Therefore, he puts effort into distorting the true message of the Gospel of Jesus Christ. Churches, for example, may be a means to do so—and with success! Some churches may proclaim the truth, but others do not at all. In general, churches or denominations are the creators of religion, and they often try to have a kind of monopoly on faith, the way of salvation, and so on. But do not let yourself be deceived. Jesus is the only way! It will never be an institution whatsoever!

Religion is kind of a framework belonging to and being created by a specific church. A major risk of such religious frameworks is to consciously or unconsciously manipulate people in this or that way. For example, a framework may imply that you are a Christian if you follow church rules, traditions, and try to avoid doing certain things. Churches may even place a burden on you by telling you, for instance, that regular church service attendance is somehow a requirement, or even a sign to be considered as a true Christian. Communion with believers is important indeed, but it has nothing to do with salvation.

Salvation is offered in Christ in spite of what you do! It is merely a question of accepting or rejecting the gift of eternal life that has already been provided through Christ's redemptive work. Thousands of people go astray, because they follow rules not of God, but of men. It is my prayer that you follow Jesus Christ alone, the way and the truth and the life, and the voice of the holy Spirit speaking to your spirit. Be aware of churches that do not proclaim assurance of salvation for those who are in Christ. Instead, they spread uncertainty concerning your salvation. For example, they relate your salvation with your level of knowledge. Once you reach a certain level of knowledge, however it is defined, you may possibly reach the point of being saved . . . as if knowledge has something to do with salvation! Never!

It is the truth, not the knowledge, that sets you free to be free indeed. There is only power in the wonderful name of Jesus Christ, who is worthy of praise and honor!

> Follow Christ and the voice of the holy Spirit dwelling in you.

Focusing on Christ

The impact of having assurance is manifested and visible in your life, your lifestyle, your

Do not foster negative feelings— sooner or later, they will manifest in your life.

preferences, and so forth. Examples of these manifestations are joy, true happiness, peace of mind, and the ability to fully rest in Jesus and his accomplished work of redemption.

However, there might be times you may feel guilty or unworthy to receive God's forgiveness because of certain activities in your current life. You might be frustrated that you have committed a specific kind of sin over and over again, and thus have feelings of shame, guilt, and being separated from God. You may feel as if you were miles away from God. Do not foster such kind of feelings!

It is about time to stop focusing on you and your situation that you may be in. Instead, consciously start focusing on Jesus Christ and his achievements for you. He laid down his life so that you may live in him! Through faith, you have full access to the grace of God. Dare to talk to God and ask him for the holy Spirit. Dare to ask him to open your eyes to see in a spiritual way. Approach God *with confidence* despite your current feelings! Focus on Christ alone.

No condemnation: members of God's household

Without Christ we are sinners, for "all have sinned, and come short of the glory of God." (Romans 3:23) Without Christ we are under the dominion of sin, strangers from the covenants of promise, excluded from eternal life, "having no hope." (Ephesians 2:12) That is the reality of one's life without Christ: eternal condemnation, which God does *not* want you to receive. Instead, "he gave his only begotten Son, that whosoever believeth in him should not perish, but have everlasting life." (John 3:16) God's motivation is love, for he *is* love. "There is therefore now no condemnation to them which are in Christ Jesus." (Romans 8:1) What does it say? The reason God sent his Son into the world is not to "condemn the world; but that the world through him might be saved." (John 3:17) This is good news, my friends! God is on our side.

Without Christ we are strangers to the covenants of promise, but "now in Christ Jesus ye who sometimes were far off are made nigh by the blood of Christ." (Ephesians 2:13) Furthermore, "now therefore ye are no more strangers and foreigners, but fellowcitizens with the saints, and of the household of God." (Ephesians 2:19) In Christ we are members of the household of God. The Apostle Paul is talking in present tense. We *are* members. The membership begins in the very moment you have been born again. The power of Jesus Christ is real and makes the impossible possible: "For what the law could not do, in that it was weak through the flesh, God sending his own Son in the likeness of sinful flesh, and for sin, condemned sin in the flesh." (Romans 8:3) Jesus condemned sin in *his* flesh. Why? "That the righteousness of the law might be fulfilled in us." (Romans 8:4) This is a powerful statement. It indirectly says that the righteousness of the law cannot be fulfilled by yourself. Therefore, Jesus is your righteousness!

No condemnation: children of God

Whatever you do or do not do, you remain in your sin unless you receive Christ into your life. *In* Christ the righteousness of the law is fulfilled in you, and you are now a child of God,

In Christ you *are* a new creature in the spirit.

an heir of the eternal inheritance. Together, we declare that Jesus "is our peace." (Ephesians 2:14)

Before having received Christ through faith and experienced the spiritual regeneration, we "were by nature the children of wrath, even as others" (Ephesians 2:3) for "as by one man sin entered into the world, and death by sin; and so death passed upon all men, for that all have sinned." (Romans 5:12) But God gave us "exceeding great and precious promises: that by these ye might be partakers of the divine nature, having escaped the corruption that is in the world through lust." (2 Peter 1:4)

Did you hear that? In Christ your very *nature* has been changed: by nature you were a child of wrath, but being washed by the blood of Jesus, you are now a partaker of the divine nature! In Christ you are "a new creature: old things are passed away; behold, all things are become new." (2 Corinthians 5:17)

You are a new creation in Christ through the washing of regeneration being born of water and of the Spirit. This is assurance of salvation, because being a partaker of the divine nature through personally accepting Jesus and his redemptive work on Calvary is equivalent to having eternal life. Paul commented: "And if Christ be in you, the body is dead because of sin; but the Spirit is life because of righteousness. But if the Spirit of him that raised up Jesus from the dead dwell in you, he that raised up Christ from the dead shall also quicken your mortal bodies by his Spirit that dwelleth in you." (Romans 8:10, 11) If the spirit of the heavenly Father dwells in you, he will raise you up from the dead in the same manner God raised up Christ. Trust in God's promise!

No condemnation: sealed with the holy Spirit

Listen! It is not you, but the holy Spirit that is the guarantee to preserve you till the second coming of Christ. "In whom ye also trusted, after that ye heard the word of truth, the gospel of your salvation: in whom also after that ye believed, ye were sealed with that holy Spirit of promise." (Ephesians 1:13) The holy Spirit is given you as the seal of God! Therefore, you can be sure of your salvation after receiving Christ and dwelling in his presence. The holy Spirit has been given to you as seal of the living God, preserving you till Christ's return.

Your true nature in Christ: holiness

One of the most astounding and mind-blowing statements about who you are in Christ is quoted by John in his first epistle: "Herein is our love made perfect, that we may have boldness in the day of judgment: because as he is, so are we in this world." (1 John 4:17) Please pay attention to the second part of this sentence. It says that we are as Jesus *is*. This is not only a reality once we are with the Lord in heaven and then on the new earth, respectively, but even in *this* world!

God does not do things by halves. "For by one offering he hath perfected for ever them that are sanctified." (Hebrews 10:14) In other words, through the sacrifice of Christ, God made perfect those who are being made holy. Are we perfect? Yes, in Christ we *are* perfect, because "we have been made holy through the sacrifice of the body of Jesus Christ once for all." (Hebrews 10:10) We are *made* holy through the sacrifice of Jesus Christ! This is passive voice—you are made holy! Do not be deceived by anybody telling you that your holiness is something you need to achieve or work for! This could not be farther from the truth. Holiness can be *received* solely through the work of Christ. It is nothing that can be earned in any way, except by believing in the Son of God and his sacrifice that saved you and me from the bondage of sin. Paul is absolutely clear about it. "But we all, with open face beholding as in a glass the glory of the Lord, are changed into the same image from glory to glory, even as by the Spirit of the Lord." (2 Corinthians 3:18) Again, passive voice is used to explain what is happening with those who are in Christ: They are changed into the same image by the Spirit of the Lord.

> Christ is the key to your new nature, which is holy, righteous, and perfect.

It is not a matter of how hard you try to become a better person, or even a better Christian, but it is a question of whether or not you have surrendered your life to Christ and opened your heart for his Spirit! After you received Christ, it is then that the Spirit transforms your life and spirit in Christ's image. It is a promise of God to change your life completely. Therefore, you can absolutely be sure of your salvation, because it is not based on your performance, but on God's power and his work! Simply believe it and put away the tormenting doubts of uncertainty concerning your salvation, and humbly receive the Gospel of God's grace in Christ!

I deeply encourage you to embrace this message of joy and freedom from doubt and uncertainty. Well, you might be thinking that the sacrifice of Christ was merely a symbolic act and so cannot make us perfect or give us a new being. Let me tell you something straightaway in the words of the Apostle Paul: "Knowing this, that our old man is crucified with him, that the body of sin might be destroyed, that henceforth we should not serve sin." (Romans 6:6) Christ has been crucified, and our old nature is crucified with him. Thus, the death of Christ and his resurrection are willingly accomplished for the sake of our inability to get free from sin. Because of Christ and his work of redemption, it is possible for everyone to get rid of sin and their sinful nature. This means that we will not receive the wages of sin, that is death. In Christ alone the old nature is exchanged with the divine one!

The key to a new nature: Jesus Christ

How is the old nature transformed to the new one? In Christ alone. This is what Paul told the Ephesians as well. "And that ye put on the new man, which after God is created in righteousness and true holiness." (Ephesians 4:24) Please read that verse again. What does it say? It says nothing less than that: the new nature is created after God in Christ, both in righteousness and true holiness. Accept the fact that in Christ you are made holy, righteous, and perfect. This is what Jesus told us to be in the Gospel according to Matthew: "Be ye therefore perfect, even as your Father which is in heaven is perfect." (Matthew 5:48) In Christ we are perfect in exactly the same way.

Furthermore, in Christ, we are made the righteousness of God. "For he hath made him to be sin for us, who knew no sin; that we might be made the righteousness of God in him." (2 Corinthians 5:21) Thus, being in Christ means to be *considered* as being the righteousness of God.

Let us never forget what we are in Christ. "For we are his workmanship, created in Christ Jesus unto good works." (Ephesians 2:10) By receiving Christ through faith by God's grace, we are created in Jesus—we are his workmanship. We are a new creation. What did God proclaim about his creation after having created the first man and the first woman? He declared his work to be *very good*. Likewise, God declares our new nature in Christ as holy, righteous, and perfect—which is indeed very good! Isn't that great news!

Being a child of God: no more fear

Those who became God's children (John 1:12), born of water and of the Spirit (John 3:5), believing in Jesus Christ (John 3:16), are heirs of the promises of God (Romans 8:17) such as eternal life (1 John 5:13), future inhabitants of the heavenly places in the heavenly Father's house (John 14:2) and ultimately, heirs of the new earth. (Revelation 21:1-7) As a born-again person, as a child of God, you do not have to fear anything. "There is no fear in love." (1 John 4:18) The price for sin has been paid by the blood of Jesus. "For ye are bought with a price: therefore glorify God in your body, and in your spirit, which are God's." (1 Corinthians 6:20)

As "the temple of the Holy Ghost which is in you, which ye have of God" (1 Corinthians 6:19) you are the property of God. You truly belong to him. Hence, you will be preserved till the end of this world by having the seal of God, which is the holy Spirit. In Christ you are not a slave of sin anymore. In addition to being "the children of God by faith in Christ Jesus" (Galatians 3:26), we are called friends of Jesus. (John 15:15) And Jesus demonstrated the greatest love toward us— he died for his friends so that they may live. "Greater love hath no man than this, that a man lay down his life for his friends." (John 15:3)

Each one of us who receive Christ through faith is a member of the body of Christ. "Now ye are the body of Christ, and members in particular." (1 Corinthians 12:27) You belong to the body of Christ, and thus to Christ in particular. You are *his* property. Jesus will not cast you out. He has bought you with a price—his shed blood on Calvary hill. What a faithful friend we have in Jesus Christ!

Jesus did everything to save us, and also equipped us with all possible blessings from above and, most of all, the holy Spirit, who is the seal of God. If we believe in Jesus and know *he* who is the way the truth and the life, our citizenship has changed drastically. "For our conversation is in heaven; from whence also we look for the Saviour, the Lord Jesus Christ: Who shall change our vile body, that it may be fashioned like unto his glorious body, according to the working whereby he is able even to subdue all things unto himself." (Philippians 3:20, 21) Jesus made us heirs of the heavenly places and has already changed our citizenship.

Recognize your identity in Christ! You are a new creation, a child of God, an heir of eternal promises. Assurance of salvation is found by believing in the mighty name of Jesus Christ and his promises. "For by grace are ye saved through faith; and that not of yourselves: it is the gift of God: Not of works, lest any man should boast." (Ephesians 2:8, 9)

Faith alone!
Unbelievers, hypocrites, Pharisees, and those who have not yet received Christ cannot understand the meaning of being

saved by grace through faith alone. The holy Spirit does not dwell in those people who have not experienced the spiritual regeneration. Thus, they are not able to discern on a spiritual level. God sent his Son Jesus Christ to save mankind, *because* we were, are, and never will be able to save ourselves by our works and personal endeavors, respectively. We cannot get rid of our sinful nature just by omitting certain sins or adopting a so-called Christian lifestyle.

> You cannot get rid of your sinful nature just by adopting a so-called Christian lifestyle.

Individual sins are not our major problem. It is sin itself that needs to be dealt with. And Jesus Christ dealt with sin at its core, condemned it in his flesh, and took away its strength.

By the power of Jesus we can experience a total transformation of our mind and nature in the spiritual regeneration and become partakers of the divine nature again! That is the Gospel! God offers his grace to all mankind. People's reaction to God's grace, however, is either to receive or reject it. In fact, many people reject the grace of God, because they do not want to admit that it is impossible for them to add something to their salvation. They think they can make it at least partially on their own. Therefore, they tend to emphasize their works and doings, even "in the name of the Lord." But the truth is, they are selfish and deny the grace of God. It is very difficult for them to believe and trust in God.

We need to surrender fully to God to manifest the fruit of the Spirit. Let us trust in God's words: "My grace is sufficient for you, for my power is made perfect in weakness." (2 Corinthians 12:9) God's grace is sufficient! The truth is that everybody can be saved by grace alone "with the precious blood of Christ, as of a lamb without blemish and without spot." (1 Peter 1:19) The decisive factor is grace, the grace of God in Jesus Christ.

What about works?

Works are not bad or wrong. A true born-again Christian naturally wants to do the will of God, because the holy Spirit urges the person to do so. This is well expressed by David's proclamation: "I delight to do thy will, O my God: yea, thy law is within my heart." (Psalms 40:8) It is very natural for our new nature in Christ that we want to do the will of God. Listen to what Jesus says: "If ye love me, keep my commandments." (John 14:15) Keeping the commandments is based upon love.

> Works cannot save you, but they will surely manifest in your new life.

If you do not love Christ, you will also not love to do what he wants you to do. But once you do love Jesus, you automatically want to do whatever he commands you to do! Doing the will of God is by no means a burden of any kind, but your delight! Ask yourself if you really love to do what the Savior of the world is telling you through God's word and the holy Spirit, who is dwelling in you.

You need to know that works cannot save you, but works will manifest in your life as a natural consequence of being born again of water and of the Spirit. Being born again, you do not need to force yourself to do the will of God in order to be a "proper Christian," but you *will do* the works that have already been prepared by God for those who become born-again followers of Christ. (Ephesians 2:10)

The works you accomplish are in fact not your own

works, but God's works! For instance, think about the seed of an apple, and ask yourself the question: What happens if you properly plant and water it? After a while, the seed will turn into a little plant and grow bigger and bigger. Finally, you will have your own apple tree and enjoy its fruits. What kind of fruits will be found on that tree? Apples, of course! Remember, "For whatsoever a man soweth, that shall he also reap." (Galatians 6:7) This is a universal law. So it is with your works. The works are the fruit of the Spirit, not your own accomplishments to be proud of! If you have not yet received the holy Spirit, you will never manifest those works that God has already prepared for you.

Unfortunately, many people pretend to have works in order to boast, or as a result of another selfish motivation. But *pretending* to have good works is as pointless as hanging bananas on an apple tree! Even if you put another variety of apples on *your* apple tree, it will never be the *source* of those fruits.

Likewise, if you imitate the fruit of the Spirit, its manifestations will never be the ones that originate from the one true source that is Jesus himself. Sooner or later the fraud will be exposed. "Not every one that saith unto me, 'Lord, Lord,' shall enter into the kingdom of heaven; but he that doeth the will of my Father which is in heaven. Many will say to me in that day, 'Lord, Lord, have we not prophesied in thy name? and in thy name have cast out devils? and in thy name done many wonderful works?' And then will I profess unto them, 'I never knew you: depart from me, ye that work iniquity.' " (Matthew 7:21-23) Obviously, it is possible to call Jesus Lord, and even do works in the name of Jesus, and nevertheless be lost. Why? Because those works were mere selfish imitations and not the works God has provided for the believers in Christ.

Apparently, works are by no means a guarantee to receive salvation. Thus, if you just try to do the will of God to play it safe so to speak, you will surely fail! By your personal endeavors, you cannot "produce" good works, nor bear true fruits that will be accepted by God. Good fruits are a natural consequence of having received Christ. It is when the fruit of the holy Spirit is initiated to manifest in your life with works that originate from the one true source, God.

> Do not try to do the will of God just to play it safe. You will surely fail.

The truth enables good works

Let us have a short look at the fundamental intention of God toward his creation. It is well summarized in the following statement: "Who will have all men to be saved, and to come unto the knowledge of the truth." (1 Timothy 2:4) God wants to save all mankind from the consequences of sin that entered the world some thousands of years ago. And, indeed, God took action and sent "his own Son in the likeness of sinful flesh, and for sin, condemned sin in the flesh: that the righteousness of the law might be fulfilled in us, who walk not after the flesh, but after the Spirit." (Romans 8:3, 4) The accusing momentum of sin in your life has been stopped by receiving Christ as Savior and Lord.

Jesus "is faithful and just to forgive us our sins, and to cleanse us from all unrighteousness." (1 John 1:9) And in Christ you are righteous! Thus, you do not need to do something in order to *get* righteous. Why? Because you are already *made* righteous by the blood of Christ and his redemptive work.

The key to salvation is to receive Christ in your life! Likewise, the will of God will have its manifestations in your life once you come to Jesus and receive him through faith. God wants men to be saved, and to come unto the knowledge of the truth. And the truth, Jesus Christ, sets you free from sin and enables you to do the will of God! You will no longer do the will of God in order to *get* saved, but because you are *already* saved in Christ! Do not forget these words of truth!

Good fruit, evil fruit

God wants you to be free from sin and start living the righteous life he has already provided for you in Christ. However, how can you bear the fruits that will not be rejected by Jesus? Hear the very words of the divine Master himself: "Even so every good tree bringeth forth good fruit; but a corrupt tree bringeth forth evil fruit. A good tree cannot bring forth evil fruit, neither can a corrupt tree bring forth good fruit. Every tree that bringeth not forth good fruit is hewn down, and cast into the fire. Wherefore by their fruits ye shall know them." (Matthew 7:17-20) The answer is simply this: You need to be a good tree to bring forth good fruit that will not be rejected by Jesus. An evil tree is not able to bear any good fruit. However, a good tree cannot bring forth evil fruit. The word "cannot" is used on purpose. If you are a good tree, you will for sure bring forth good fruit, and it is impossible for you to bring forth evil fruit.

For illustrative purposes, examine the apple tree. What kind of fruit does it bear? Your answer may be *apples*. And you are absolutely right! It is natural that an apple tree bears apples, like a fig tree will grow figs. Nobody is wondering why or complaining that an apple tree bears apples.

Likewise, born-again Christians will bring forth good fruit. This is simply a *natural* consequence, because a born-again Christian bears the fruit of the Spirit, not his or her own. You can think of the holy Spirit as the seed that was metaphorically put in your heart. Now you do not need to guess which fruit will start to grow within you. It is the good fruit, namely the fruit of the Spirit which is "love, joy, peace, longsuffering, gentleness, goodness, faith, meekness, temperance." (Galatians 5:22, 23) Is it *your* fruit? Surely not! It is the fruit of the Spirit.

> The holy Spirit is like the divine seed put in your heart. Its fruit will surely manifest in your life.

The holy Spirit dwelling in you will change and transform your life in any respect. It is just natural! These manifestations of the fruit of the Spirit will for certain show up in your life! Not because you will try hard to bring forth at least some buds, but because of the work of the holy Spirit in you!

Through faith, you have access to God's grace and so to the spiritual reality of salvation in Christ. By grace, God has provided everything for your salvation—the redemptive work through Christ and the holy Spirit as the one who guides you into all truth and ensures spiritual growth, specifically to bear the fruit of the Spirit.

The crucial difference: true faith, good works

James proclaimed: "Even so faith, if it hath not works, is

dead, being alone." (James 2:17) This is some kind of definition of biblical faith. True faith will bring forth works of righteousness according to God's promises. Does it say that you need to "produce" works? No! Be careful in your words. You do not *need* to produce works, and especially not your own works, but you *will have* works! This is *the* crucial difference! Faith in Jesus will bring forth the fruit of the Spirit, because the seed of the Spirit will come to growth in your life as a natural process.

No boasting, no selfish pride

There is absolutely no room for boasting, or being proud of any good works that manifest in your life. Why? Because it is Jesus who lives in you once you received him and accomplishes every good work in you. As a matter of fact, your works are his works. You can be "confident of this very thing, that he which hath begun a good work in you will perform it until the day of Jesus Christ." (Philippians 1:6) Christ began the work in you and will perform it till he returns the second time.

Furthermore, Paul points out: "I am crucified with Christ: nevertheless I live; yet not I, but Christ liveth in me: and the life which I now live in the flesh I live by the faith of the Son of God, who loved me, and gave himself for me." (Galatians 2:20) Who accomplished the works in Paul's life? It was Jesus who gave himself for Paul, for you, for me, and for the entirety of mankind. "For God so loved the world, that he gave his only begotten Son, that whosoever believeth in him should not perish, but have everlasting life." (John 3:16)

The grace of God which brings forth good works in you

is a free gift in Jesus Christ. Through faith, you have access to God's bountiful grace that leads to salvation. Give it a try! It's worth a shot. I know what I am talking about.

Righteousness—not by works of the law!

Your own works cannot accomplish anything regarding salvation. Paul is very clear that righteousness cannot be obtained by works, but by faith. "For therein is the righteousness of God revealed from faith to faith: as it is written, The just shall live by faith." (Romans 1:17) It is the grace of God that makes you righteous in Christ through faith. "I do not frustrate the grace of God: for if righteousness come by the law, then Christ is dead in vain." (Galatians 2:21)

In other words, you cannot be saved by works of any kind, no matter how hard you try, or how sincere your endeavors may be. Works have nothing to do with achieving righteousness, and hence, eternal salvation. There is only one work that ends with a "it is finished" (John 19:30), namely the decisive work of Jesus Christ. Through the sacrifice of God's Son Jesus Christ you are made holy *once for all time*.

Righteousness—which one?

Let no one deceive you that it is necessary or even possible to establish your own righteousness. "For they being ignorant of God's righteousness, and going about to establish their own righteousness, have not submitted themselves unto the righteousness of God. For Christ is the end of the law for righteousness to every one that believeth. For Moses describeth the righteousness which is of the law, That the man which doeth those things shall live by them." (Romans

10:3-5) Receive God's righteousness in Christ through faith!

Falling from grace

God's grace is wonderful. It is the very expression of God's nature. Therefore, Paul warns you not to fall from grace. "Christ is become of no effect unto you, whosoever of you are justified by the law; ye are fallen from grace. For we through the Spirit wait for the hope of righteousness by faith. For in Jesus Christ neither circumcision availeth any thing, nor uncircumcision; but faith which worketh by love." (Galatians 5:4-6) It is possible to fall from grace. The one who tries to be justified by the law indirectly rejects the free gift of salvation in Christ, and so doing falls from grace. Justification is not by works but by faith alone. Which kind of faith is meant according to Paul's inspired statement? It is the faith that brings forth works and expresses itself in love. Concerning works, it is not about doing this or that, but allowing the seed of the holy Spirit to come to growth in your life. All manifestations of good works in your life are the work of the holy Spirit, not yours at all.

> When it comes to salvation, falling from grace means to put your trust in your own abilities.

Bringing good fruit—abide in Jesus!

A good tree brings forth good fruit. In Christ you are a good tree, so to speak. How can you remain good and in a state where you bear good fruit? Jesus, "the true vine" (John 15:1), says: "Abide in me, and I in you. As the branch cannot bear fruit of itself, except it abide in the vine; no more can ye, except ye abide in me. I am the vine, ye are the branches: He that abideth in me, and I in him, the same bringeth forth much fruit: for without me ye can do nothing." (John 15:4, 5) Without Christ you can do nothing, but with him, you bring forth fruit galore.

Conclusion: stop fearing, start trusting in Jesus!

Put your trust in Jesus Christ and his redemptive work of salvation. In Christ you are a child of God who will not be condemned, but will inherit eternal life. You do not need to be afraid of the great day of the Lord at all. You might be worrying about being unprepared, or rather, unworthy. In Christ you are not unprepared or unworthy, but an heir of the things to come. Do not let doubts flood your thoughts!

Ask yourself why you might be afraid of the coming of our Savior and Lord Jesus Christ. May it be that you put the assurance of salvation into your own hands? Do you at least partially want or have the urge to add something to Christ's work of redemption? Do you look upon your life and realize that, however much you have tried, you still have not succeeded in being holy and living a Christian life according to the will of God? What is it that produces fear in your life? Is it that you "have sinned, and come short of the glory of God"? (Romans 3:23) Without Christ we all come short of the glory of God. That is true. But God loves us and sent his Son Jesus Christ to destroy the work of the devil. And whosoever believes in Jesus is free from sin and his or her sinful nature.

> Putting your trust in Jesus Christ will manifest in a satisfying life.

You might have been struggling for years to know whether you are saved or not. You may try hard to meet

God's standard, but still fail miserably. You may not feel comfortable in your spiritual life. Are you satisfied, or still struggling with the question: Am I saved? Remember, you do not need to accomplish works in order to be saved or have assurance of salvation. On the contrary, you need to rest from your own works and let God work in you through the holy Spirit!

Conclusion: a settled spiritual life

The question is, how can you live a settled spiritual life that is not work-oriented? How can you have assurance of salvation in Christ? First, accept the truth that your works have no power to contribute to your salvation—not by works, but by grace you are saved. Second, you need to understand the relationship between grace and works. God's grace is available for the humble. "God resisteth the proud, but giveth grace unto the humble." (James 4:6) Grace is already there and can be received through faith. Works, however, are a natural consequence of that faith. Faith is followed by works, not the other way round. Likewise, you do not need to have any works in order to get saved, but once you are saved by grace, good works will abundantly come forth naturally by the power of the holy Spirit dwelling in you.

Conclusion: salvation is a free gift of God

Glory to Jesus Christ who saved us through his sacrifice! Salvation is a free gift from God, because we would have never been able to get rid of our sinful nature by any kind of works and thus obtain peace of mind. Will *you* receive God's gift of eternal life in Christ through faith? It surely is the only way to God! And once you have experienced true freedom in

Christ, you will *never* thirst again. This is a promise from Jesus himself! You cannot add anything to your salvation.

In Christ you do not need to be afraid in any respect, because God loves you more than you can ever imagine! In Christ you are saved by grace through faith. You do not need to show any works to get accepted by Jesus. Salvation is a gift of God! Remember, without Christ "we are all as an unclean thing, and all our righteousnesses are as filthy rags." (Isaiah 64:6) But *after* you have received Jesus in your life through faith, good works that God has already provided for you will naturally show up as a consequence of the holy Spirit bringing forth his fruit in you.

Conclusion: the good shepherd

The amazing parable of the good shepherd summarizes the essential aspects of assurance of salvation and clearly points out that assurance of salvation is a reality in Christ our Savior and Lord. In Christ, you can be sure of your salvation, not because of you being so "great" or living a good Christian lifestyle—at least you try to do so—but because of the precious blood of Jesus Christ shed for the sins of the world.

Jesus says: "I am the good shepherd: the good shepherd giveth his life for the sheep." (John 10:11) Jesus unambiguously defines his position with respect to the sheep. *He* is the good shepherd and takes care of his sheep, even if it means death! Who are the sheep? Metaphorically speaking, those who have received Christ by grace through faith represent *his* sheep.

> Jesus Christ has come that we might have life more abundantly. Receive Christ and experience this reality!

Besides *his* sheep, there are also sheep that do not belong to Christ. Peter, for example, uses the word sheep as a metaphor for people. "For ye were as sheep going astray; but are now returned unto the Shepherd and Bishop of your souls." (1 Peter 2:25) People who have not yet received Christ are like sheep going astray. But once they return to the shepherd, they are given a fruitful and satisfying life and, most of all, they remain on track. They do not need to go astray again, because they have found *the* way, *the* truth, and *the* life! In contrast to the hireling, Jesus is willing to care, and even die, for his sheep. He truly identifies himself with his flock.

Jesus, the good shepherd, came to this world to accomplish the work of salvation, which comprises the following aspect: "I am come that they might have life, and that they might have it more abundantly." (John 10:10) Jesus came to this world so that we have life in him. Without Christ there is no life whatsoever. In particular, his purpose was and still is to give us a rich and satisfying life. The assurance of salvation is built on the foundation of the redemptive work of Christ.

Jesus accomplished everything so that we might remain untouched of eternal condemnation, which is the wages of sin. Through faith in Jesus Christ we receive salvation and eternal life, which is the gift of God.

Jesus, the "KING OF KINGS, AND LORD OF LORDS" (Revelation 19:16) is the only one who is worthy and able to declare: "It is finished." (John 19:30) It was on the cross at Calvary where the Son of God died "for the sins of the whole world." (1 John 2:2)

The death of Jesus is an invitation of life for us! And his

resurrection serves as our justification! Paul states the wonderful truth while talking about Jesus: "Who was delivered for our offences, and was raised again for our justification." (Romans 4:25) This is good news. This is the Gospel of Jesus Christ. This is what John 3:16 is all about. It is about Jesus Christ, who assures you fervently: "the one who comes to Me I will by no means cast out." (John 6:37)

4: What Shall I Do?

In today's society, unfortunately, *even* in a Christian setting, you need to put something forward in order to *be* someone. This mindset typically starts to impact your childhood and continues to manipulate your mind well into adulthood. The baseline you find is something like, You *are* someone, if you have achieved something in your life. For example, people may esteem you in a special way because you have attended university and achieved some academic degrees. Others may adore your musical abilities, because you have worked hard on your musical perfectionism. If you have made a lot of money, you may earn admiring, or even envious, glances. Hence, if you have achieved something, people have a special focus on you that puts you in the spotlight. Those examples are not bad in themselves, but the mindset around those things may turn into an *ego boost*.

Even on a spiritual level, people may try to achieve something in order to reach a certain level of spirituality. In order to *become* a highly spiritual person, they think that they need to do or accomplish something—for instance, you need to meditate more, pray more, do this or that. Consequently, their pathway to spiritual enlightenment is characterized especially by the following thinking pattern: you need to do something in order to become something in order to finally be someone. Who is the center of this mindset? It is you, and it tells you the following: *You* are responsible and particularly able to change yourself. *You* are the one who has the ability to become a greater spiritual being. This mindset is all about *you*. Unfortunately, this kind of mindset is not in harmony with God's will, but obviously, it found its way into Christianity and caused much damage. Jesus shall be the center of your life!

Religion does not help, but Jesus does!

Religion tells you that God loves you, but simultaneously, it bars the way to a healthy idea of God. "You are exaggerating!" you may say. But let us face the truth. There are millions of Christians who have a distorted picture of God in their minds. They do believe in God and regularly attend church services, but they are not convinced of the existence of eternal life, of a *loving* God, of salvation, and so on. Their lives are full of sorrow, uncertainty, fear, and physical, as well as mental, diseases of all kind. They doubt their acceptance by God. They doubt they are good enough in Christ to escape the fire of hell. Depression and unhappiness are the natural consequences in a life full of uncertainty and, consequently, fear!

There is no manifestation of the fruit of the Spirit in their lives, even though the Apostle Paul is talking about a natural consequence in a born-again Christian's life to bring forth the fruit of the Spirit. Oh yes, religion has mostly destroyed the idea of a loving and caring God! Invitingly, it proclaims that God loves you, that God cares for you, that God did everything to save you, and so on. However, these statements are followed by a restrictive *but*. For example, God loves you, *but* only if you follow his word, or God did everything to save you, *but*, of course, you need to do your part and add some good works, like generous donations, volunteer work, and attending church service on a regular basis. Religion may tell you that you can freely come to Christ, but once you are with Christ, it imposes burdens on your spiritual life: sticking to certain church rules, traditions, laws, or urging you to do this or that, and hence, making your life a spiritual torture. It is focusing on works and not on the finished work of Christ!

> Christ is enough. Trust in him alone!

Religion is proclaiming the opposite of what Paul says: "For if, when we were enemies, we were reconciled to God by the death of his Son, much more, being reconciled, we shall be saved by *his* life." (Romans 5:8-10) You were a sinner, but you were reconciled by the death of Jesus Christ. In particular, it says that being reconciled to God by the blood of Jesus, you do not need to fear anything, because you shall be saved by Jesus' life all the more!

Moreover, religion may even try to imitate the work of the holy Spirit and so the work of sanctification. Instead of letting the holy Spirit work in you and bring forth the fruit of the Spirit, religion tends to play it safe by setting all kinds of regulations, commandments, prohibitions, dogmas, and so forth to press people into a kind of "godly" scheme. But there is a major problem with these rules and provisions: They are mere outward appearances, with no power to change a person's nature or heart.

In fact, some religious people may be familiar with Christ, but they do not actually know him, and hence, are "giving heed to seducing spirits, and doctrines of devils." (1 Timothy 4:1) Sanctification is not a work done by you, but *in* you by the holy Spirit.

Works do not help either!

The Apostle Paul warns us insistently: "For the time will come when they will not endure sound doctrine; but after their own lusts shall they heap to themselves teachers, having itching ears; and they shall turn away their ears from the truth, and shall be turned unto fables." (2 Timothy 4:3, 4) The law of God and all the regulations and commands have never had the power to save us from sin, otherwise Jesus Christ would have died in vain! But they did point to Jesus, the Savior, as *the* solution to becoming righteous again. "For Christ is the end of the law for righteousness to every one that believeth." (Romans 10:4) Rely on Jesus and let the holy Spirit change you step by step, according to God's will!

> Put away your self-centered mindset. Instead, put Jesus first!

Therefore, any religion, church, or whoever focuses on works in order to receive salvation is from the devil. Why? Because it puts *you* in the center of salvation instead of Christ. To be honest, it deeply shames God and his unconditional love for his creatures and the redemptive work of Jesus Christ, our Savior and Lord.

Jesus Christ died for us while we were yet sinners. He accomplished the work of salvation for those who were even enemies. "For if, when we were enemies, we were reconciled to God by the death of his Son." (Romans 5:10) It is the death of Jesus Christ that reconciled us to God! At that time, when Jesus victoriously proclaimed that it is finished and accomplished the work of salvation, we did not even exist! Think about it! Jesus died for all sins that were committed, are committed, and even *will be* committed.

Now, who is the center of *this* mindset? It is Jesus Christ, the Son of man! This time, there is no *but* and no uncertainty. It is not by your works, but it is the grace of God that saves you in Christ, through faith. "I do not frustrate the grace of God: for if righteousness come by the law, then Christ is dead in vain." (Galatians 2:21)

What shall I do to be saved? Believe!

Thinking that salvation is something dependent on you inevitably imposes an unbearable burden on your shoulders—when is enough really enough to reach the level of salvation? There is uncertainty, and fear may implacably pop up in your mind and in your life. And fear limits your degree of freedom! You can try to at least *feel* that you have achieved enough to literally earn the kingdom of God. But you will never know if *your* enough is equivalent to God's enough.

It is then that the nagging question arises: *What shall I do to be saved?* And it is definitely a legitimate question. There might be some religions, churches, or people trying to tackle this question who stutter when trying to give suitable answers. However, you have to know that these questions of when is enough truly enough and what shall I do to be saved, have already been answered a long time ago. The answers are found in the blood of Jesus that was shed for you and me.

It was Jesus who did what you never would have been able to do: He paid the price for sin and came "to give his life a ransom for many." (Mark 10:45) If you believe in the Son of God, you surely receive forgiveness and eternal life!

Furthermore, in Christ you are a new creature born of the Spirit. You do not need to do anything to become a new creature, except receive Christ. In Christ you *are* already a new creation! It is not your merit. It is through faith in Jesus that you become a partaker of the divine nature. Believe it!

By grace through faith!

Even at the time of Paul, people popped up and taught that the work of Christ and receiving Jesus personally are not enough to be saved. You read this in Acts chapter 15. The apostolic council took place in Jerusalem to tackle the question of what it actually is that saves people, especially Gentiles who turned to God, from eternal condemnation. Some believers of the sect of the Pharisees claimed that the believing Gentiles needed to keep the law of Moses, especially the commandment of circumcision. One of the conclusions of this discussion was: "Now therefore why tempt ye God, to put a yoke upon the neck of the disciples, which neither our fathers nor we were able to bear? But we believe that through the grace of the Lord Jesus Christ we shall be saved, even as they." (Acts 15:10, 11)

These words are clear and easy to understand. You are not saved by keeping the law of Moses. You are saved by grace through faith in Jesus Christ.

Doing God's will: what is the underlying motivation?

There was a man who approached Jesus to ask him what

exactly he needed to do to have eternal life. Jesus immediately responded: "Thou knowest the commandments, Do not commit adultery, Do not kill, Do not steal, Do not bear false witness, Honour thy father and thy mother." (Luke 18:20) Does Jesus' answer indicate salvation through keeping the commandments? No, quite the contrary! Listen to what Jesus further answered after the man had said that he kept all these commandments from his youth up. "Yet lackest thou one thing: sell all that thou hast, and distribute unto the poor, and thou shalt have treasure in heaven: and come, follow me." (Luke 18:22) What was the man lacking in his spiritual life? It was Jesus! Apparently, the man kept the commandments, or at least he thought that he kept them. But that was not enough.

The man lacked one thing: He did not follow Jesus! The commandments of God are not wrong or bad. They are just not intended to save you from eternal condemnation! The decisive point is the underlying *motivation* of following God and his will. Do you want to live a life according to the will of God in order to kind of deserve eternal life? If so, you will certainly fail! Why? Because this is a self-centered motivation that implies that Jesus is not enough and that the price for sin has not been paid in full. However, do you want to live a life according to God's will because you personally know, trust, and want to follow Jesus? If so, you are certainly moved by the holy Spirit.

With God all things are possible

You need to get to know the truth, Jesus Christ, and *his* work of salvation, and the truth will set you free. Otherwise, you remain in your sins, and especially in your sinful nature. Even the disciples recognized that it is nearly impossible to be saved. In astonishment they uttered the question of questions: "Who then can be saved?" (Matthew 19:25) Immediately, Jesus responded: "With men this is impossible; but with God all things are possible." (Matthew 19:26) It is possible to be saved because of Jesus Christ.

> In Christ you are saved: The holy Spirit will be the driving force in your life!

You do not need to do this or that to obtain salvation. The only thing you need to do is to receive Christ in your life. And once you have received him, the holy Spirit dwells in you. Consequently, you will actually *want* to live a life that is in harmony with every aspect of God's will that has been revealed to you by the holy Spirit. To sum up, why is it that you *want* to be oriented toward the will of God in your life? It is because you *are* saved in Christ and are now a partaker of the divine nature. And the holy Spirit starts transforming your life.

You do not need to earn your salvation. Nobody needs to pay the wages of sin anymore. In fact, no one could have ever paid it except Jesus. In Christ you are saved! Thus, everything you do is not motivated by some selfish thoughts of adding to the work of salvation or the like. The motivation or driving force is, then, the holy Spirit in you: "For as many as are led by the Spirit of God, they are the sons of God." (Romans 8:14)

Having said all this, what was the man in the parable truly lacking? It was full devotion to the Lord Jesus Christ. The man obviously imitated works of righteousness without having found its source. Jesus came to this world that "we might be made the righteousness of God in him." (2

Corinthians 5:21) You are made the righteousness of God in Christ. It is passive voice! You are the receiver of salvation through faith, and Jesus is the one who accomplished it. Do not mix up the two sides of salvation!

Do you hear the voice of the good shepherd?

The crucial factor to have eternal life is to come to Christ and follow him without any compromises! The words of Jesus are very clear: "And he that taketh not his cross, and followeth after me, is not worthy of me." (Matthew 10:38) If you do not follow Jesus, the good shepherd, you are not belonging to his sheep. Why? Because Jesus "goeth before them, and the sheep follow him: for they know his voice." (John 10:4)

Only if you hear Jesus' voice are you able to follow him. And when are you able to hear his voice, and therefore follow him? It is when the holy Spirit dwells in you once you have received Christ by grace through faith. It is then that you hear God's voice: "He that is of God heareth God's words: ye therefore hear them not, because ye are not of God." (John 8:47) It is then when you bring forth the works that have already been prepared for you from your heavenly Father. Do *you* hear the voice of God, and do *you* follow Jesus unconditionally?

> Believe in the Lord Jesus Christ and be saved!

The keeper of the prison

Another occurrence described in the book of Acts is also dealing with the essential question: What must I do to be saved? Paul and Silas were imprisoned and, at midnight, they prayed and praised God. And "suddenly there was a great earthquake, so that the foundations of the prison were shaken: and immediately all the doors were opened, and every one's bands were loosed." (Acts 16:26) The keeper of the prison was awaking out of his sleep and realized the prison doors were open. Being afraid that all prisoners had fled, he decided to kill himself. But Paul assured him that all prisoners were there, and thus the keeper did not kill himself.

Instead, he turned to Paul and Silas, still trembling, fell down before them, and said, "Sirs, what must I do to be saved?" (Acts 16:30) What would your answer be? Before you start speculating, let us listen to the plain answer of Paul and Silas: "Believe on the Lord Jesus Christ, and thou shalt be saved, and thy house." (Acts 16:31) Yes, it is that simple. Please notice the equal message of John 3:16 herein! You need to believe in order to get saved. Nothing more, nothing less! Having faith in Jesus and his transforming power will change your life completely, because the holy Spirit dwells in you and enables you to follow Jesus at all costs.

The Gospel of Jesus: not enough for the proud

Proud and arrogant people may oppose the statement of being saved merely by receiving Jesus into one's life. They may insist that it is not enough, to just believe in Jesus will not enable us to receive the gift of eternal life. Those people may call it *cheap grace* or alike, even though God's word does not know this term at all. They tell you that you need to believe in God and his Son Jesus Christ, but, at the end, you also need to *do* something in order to be saved. This is a lie that mixes up the two sides of salvation. Jesus is on the giving side and provides salvation to everyone. We are on the receiving side and cannot add anything to it.

Works based on true motives are totally fine, but they do

not save you, or even add something to your own salvation. Remember, true works are a natural consequence of being saved and having a new nature in Christ! The only thing we can do is make a decision whether to receive salvation out of the hands of Jesus or not. Please notice that in order to be able to receive something, this very thing needs to be there *already*. Therefore, salvation can be received and is consequently already there and ready to be picked up, because salvation has already been accomplished through Christ alone!

God's love toward his creation

God so loved the world that he gave his only begotten Son Jesus Christ "to save that which was lost." (Matthew 18:11) In the context of this verse, Jesus uses the illustration of a man and his sheep. One sheep has gone astray. What does the man do? He is seeking the lost sheep, and when he finds it, the man rejoices a lot about having found his sheep.

Then Jesus tells us the touching truth about God's will for his creation. "Even so it is not the will of your Father which is in heaven, that one of these little ones should perish." (Matthew 18:14) Jesus assures you: "Likewise, I say unto you, there is joy in the presence of the angels of God over one sinner that repenteth." (Luke 15:10) God wants to save you, and that is why he sent his Son Jesus Christ to perfectly accomplish the work of salvation.

The Prodigal Son and the love of the Father

The love of God is emphasized even further in the parable of the so-called Prodigal Son, which is found in Luke 15:11ff. After the son had squandered his money and all his belongings, he decided to return to his father. "And he arose, and came to his father. But when he was yet a great way off, his father saw him, and had compassion, and ran, and fell on his neck, and kissed him." (Luke 15:20) Notice what this verse tells us about the love of the father for his son. The father saw his son even when he was still far away. It seems that the father had been on the lookout for his son ever since the son left him. There was no anger nor hatred, but true compassion found in the heart of the father. He ran to his son, hugged and kissed him, and proclaimed, full of joy: "this my son was dead, and is alive again; he was lost, and is found." (Luke 15:24)

> Jesus is knocking on the door of your heart. Will you let him in?

The parable is talking about our heavenly Father and shows God to be compassionate and full of mercy. Mankind literally ran, and is still running, away from God, but he is on the lookout for you and for me. Jesus himself, our good shepherd, is watching out for us. "Behold, I stand at the door, and knock: if any man hear my voice, and open the door, I will come in to him, and will sup with him, and he with me." (Revelation 3:20) Are you hearing the voice of Jesus, and will you open the door to let him in? Receive Christ in your life and become a dearly beloved child of God!

Become a child of God by receiving Christ!

It is simply a lie to think that your salvation is somehow dependent on you and your works. Jesus Christ completely accomplished the work of salvation. It is the gift of God through Jesus Christ to all mankind! And through faith, you have access to this gift of salvation. It is enough to believe in

Jesus Christ to be saved. It is the grace of God that makes it possible. To proclaim being saved in Christ is far from being proud or arrogant. A born-again person will give all the glory to Jesus Christ. No boasting at all! Once you believe in Jesus and accept his gift of salvation and redemption of sins and your sinful nature, you become a partaker of the divine nature. You are the temple of the holy Spirit who dwells and works in you. When you receive Christ through faith, thus experiencing the spiritual regeneration, then, primarily, you are saved by grace through faith. You are now belonging to the body of Christ. You are a child of God!

> Sanctification is not a measuring unit of your level of holiness. It is, rather, the ministry of the holy Spirit.

Sanctification vs. metamorphosis

The holy Spirit has been promised to mankind. He will be given by the heavenly Father to those who ask for him. The holy Spirit then continues to work in you. Paul calls this process *sanctification*, which, for instance, produces good works in your life. In particular, sanctification brings forth the fruit of the Spirit by the ministry of the holy Spirit. You literally get transformed!

Now we get to a point that is very crucial to be understood correctly: sanctification is happening once you are a child of God, once the holy Spirit dwells in you. Chronologically speaking, you first turn to God and receive Jesus Christ as Savior and Lord, and then you automatically participate in the process of sanctification through the ministry of the holy Spirit. Some people often mix up this order and put sanctification first. This could not be farther from the truth. It is a deception of Satan and an attempt to imitate the sanctification process. To reverse the order and put sanctification first is like a caterpillar who tries to fly before becoming a beautiful butterfly. It is impossible. In order to be able to fly, he first needs to be transformed to a butterfly. This process is called metamorphosis and is a structural change. The Apostle Paul also used the verb transform, which is based on the term metamorphosis. (Romans 12:2) By using this term, he indicated our need to be transformed in order to be able to discern spiritually. Metamorphosis is the transformation from a sinful nature to a partaker of the divine nature. In other words, it is the transformation from being a sinner into a child of God. This is only possible in Christ. Only in Christ can you be a new creature. In Christ you then have the holy Spirit who exerts influence on you and works the sanctification in your life. Obviously, in this context, sanctification is *not* the process of metamorphosis. Metamorphosis is the prerequisite in order to participate in the sanctification process.

> Metamorphosis comes first. Then sanctification. Do not mix up this order!

The consequences of mixing up the order of metamorphosis and sanctification are devastating. People think that they need to be sanctified first in order to be saved, and finally obtain eternal salvation. Therefore, they tend to focus on their works, and even on the works of others. They might ask themselves: Am I sanctified enough to be saved? It inevitably implicates uncertainty. They look on their lives with all their flaws and where they again missed out on being more holy and friendly, and so on. To put themselves in a better position, they start to compare themselves with others who fail even more—at least in their eyes. However, it is not really possible to come to rest, because you never know when enough is enough. Honestly speaking, it is never enough what you do on your own to obtain salvation! Like the caterpillar, you need a metamorphosis first to be able to fly! This is only possible in Christ. Only in Christ are you a new creature participating in the sanctification through the ministry of the holy Spirit. It is then you can rest from your works and be sure of your eternal destiny.

Stop comparing yourself with others!

Comparing yourself with others is always misleading, and a sign of immaturity and being unwilling to face the truth about yourself. Peter once was curious about the future of one of the disciples. Jesus answered him straightforwardly. "If I want him to remain alive until I return, what is that to you? You must follow me." (John 21:22)

The point is, as always, that you need to examine and openly ask yourself if *you* want to follow Jesus. If you are looking at others in order to justify your current, potentially sinful, position, spiritual growth is not possible at all.

Sanctification and its false application

Satan has succeeded in presenting sanctification as a means to get saved *before* Jesus has ever been received. This is a very subtle deception. This dangerous lie paralyzes sinners to come to Christ as they *are*! Satan has successfully lied to them. Let me tell you the truth: Sanctification is, per definition, not possible in a sinner's life. You need Christ *first*!

Incidentally, in Christ you are not a sinner anymore, but

righteous. You might fall into sinful habits or actions, but you deeply regret having sinned against God. You have literally been convicted by the holy Spirit. And you know that you have an advocate with the heavenly Father, namely Jesus Christ. You regret having sinned and saddened God. To really regret and be sad about your sin and individual sins is a different story than merely regretting sin and its manifestations for the sake of its predominantly negative consequences in your life.

Now, there is no such thing as sanctification in the absence of the holy Spirit, because the holy Spirit is precisely like the seed of sanctification. If there is no seed, there will not be anything that sprouts. Sanctification happens *after* you receive the gift of salvation through faith. Only a person who is born of water and of the Spirit is participating in the process of sanctification. Thus, sanctification is not the means to get saved and inherit eternal life, but it is the natural consequence of being born again of water and of the spirit.

The process of sanctification vs. having been sanctified

The Apostle Paul warned the church of God at Corinth that the unrighteous will not inherit the kingdom of God. After listing all kinds of unrighteous behavior, such as fornication, idolatry, adultery, and many more, he continues his message: "And such were some of you: but ye are washed, but ye are sanctified, but ye are justified in the name of the Lord Jesus, and by the Spirit of our God." (1 Corinthians 6:11) Paul is clearly pointing out that many members of that church at Corinth were unrighteous people. But he declared that they *were* these kind of people. However, now they *are* washed, sanctified, and justified in the name of the Lord Jesus Christ and by the holy Spirit. Paul is telling them that they *are* sanctified. In this context, sanctified means separated from profane things and dedicated to God. And this separation happened after they had received Christ! In fact, once you are saved, on the one hand, you are already sanctified in the sense of being separated from profane things and dedicated to God. On the other hand, you will be sanctified even further through the power of the holy Spirit living in you. In the latter case we are talking about the process of sanctification. In fact, sanctification becomes reality once you are born again.

> Sanctification is the process of eliminating your love for sin, and even the tendency to flirt with sin.

Sanctification is not a process where *you* are the key actor, but God, through his Spirit. This is best illustrated with the following metaphor: "Behold, as the clay is in the potter's hand, so are ye in mine hand." (Jeremiah 18:6) God declares himself the potter caring for his clay. Your part is not to form yourself by your own endeavors, but to let yourself be formed by the potter's hand. Never mix that up!

Sanctification and your relationship to sin

One of the most obvious manifestations of sanctification in the life of a born-again person is his or her relationship with sin. If you say that you love the Lord Jesus Christ and have received him through faith, simultaneously raise the following questions to examine yourself: What does my relationship to sin look like? Do I still like or hate sin? Jesus reminds you accordingly: "If any man love the world, the love of the Father is not in him. For all that is in the world, the lust of the flesh, and the lust of the eyes, and the pride of life, is not of the Father, but is of the world." (1 John 2:15, 16) To tell you the truth, a born-again person is no longer bound under the dominion of sin, but set free from sin, its dominion and power by the blood of Jesus Christ. This freedom in Christ has drastic consequences in your life. Sin and sinful acts of any kind once loved are now truly detested by the person who experienced the spiritual regeneration. It is not the person's work or endeavor to ultimately reach a level at which he or she starts hating sin in its various manifestations—remember, you are not the potter, but the clay being formed by the potter himself! Rather, it is the new creature in Christ that has a transformed mind. This new mind finally leads to a state where sin is actually hated!

The holy Spirit dwelling in you will transform your entire being! You can and will experience this transformation literally in your life once you have received Christ through faith. This is not pure theory!

What if you fall and yield to sin?

Knowing the status of your relationship with sin will help you to examine yourself: Am I in Christ or not? But what about the fact that you sometimes may fail and behave as if you were still under the dominion of sin? Let God speak through his servant John: "If we confess our sins, he is faithful and just to forgive us our sins, and to cleanse us from all unrighteousness." (1 John 1:9) In Jesus, your sins *are* forgiven. Even your sinful nature has been nullified in Christ. No matter what you did, your sins are forgiven in Christ. But you need to confess your sins. Do not sweep your guilt under the rug, but confess and then "go, and sin no more." (John 8:11)

Jesus died for your sins and "also for the sins of the whole world." (1 John 2:2) He died for you so that you may have life! Jesus encourages you: "Let not your heart be troubled: ye believe in God, believe also in me." (John 14:1)

Baptism—washing away your sins

> Baptism does not save you. It is a natural response to those who have received Christ.

Let us once more turn to the account of Paul and Silas in prison. In this report you can find an important message that we did not focus on yet. It is the passage where Paul and Silas had an encounter with the keeper. "And they spake unto him the word of the Lord, and to all that were in his house. And he took them the same hour of the night, and washed their stripes; and was baptized, he and all his, straightway. And when he had brought them into his house, he set meat before them, and rejoiced, believing in God with all his house." (Acts 16:32-34) Paul and Silas were preaching the word of the Lord to the keeper and all who were in that house.

What happened after they had spoken to the keeper and his family? They all believed and rejoiced! Moreover, the keeper and his family were baptized. The natural response of those who want to follow him and have come to faith in Jesus is the urge to get *baptized*, because God simply said to do so. "Repent, and be baptized every one of you in the name of Jesus Christ for the remission of sins, and ye shall receive the gift of the Holy Ghost." (Acts 2:38) People are baptized not because any religious system, church, spiritual group, or leader has demanded baptism, but because God himself mandated it and put it in every heart that has been converted to Jesus Christ.

In its Greek origin the verb to baptize means to immerse, to wash, to make clean with water, or even to bathe. Sin is like dirt, and we need to be washed, baptized, in order to be clean. Does it say that baptism is mandatory to get cleansed from sin? No, because baptism without prior repentance and faith in the cleansing blood of Jesus Christ is nothing more than a mere external act.

Religion may tend to make baptism a question of salvation and exploit it for their benefit. Churches assume authority to state that you only become a proper member of God's family through baptism—*even* if you have already received Christ! That is a major error, because Jesus himself said that once you belong to him, you are his sheep *already*! It is then that you *want* to be baptized in the name of Jesus!

Remember the occurrence of the crucifixion. One of the malefactor asked Jesus to remember him once Jesus entered his kingdom. This was his expression of faith. He was not baptized, but Jesus nevertheless assured him of being saved! Thus, baptism is obviously not a necessity to be saved, but rather, a godly inspired urge and personal act of expressing faith in Jesus Christ and his work of redemption through his death and resurrection. "Know ye not, that so many of us as were baptized into Jesus Christ were baptized into his death? Therefore we are buried with him by baptism into death: that like as Christ was raised up from the dead by the glory of the Father, even so we also should walk in newness of life." (Romans 6:3, 4)

Baptism—being a member of the body of Christ
Many churches interpret the word of God for the sake of

emphasizing that *their* church is the true church here on earth. So it is done with the following verse that Peter once registered: "Then they that gladly received his word were baptized: and the same day there were added unto them about three thousand souls." (Acts 2:41) Peter preached the Gospel unto the people, and some of them received the word of God and were baptized. Three thousand souls were added on this day. What had they been added to? The answer is provided some verses later. "And the Lord added to the church daily such as should be saved." (Acts 2:46)

Here, at the latest, religion comes into play, telling you that all those people are baptized automatically into some kind of local church! This is not what the text is actually telling us. It simply states that they have been added to the *church*. Period! Thus, from this text only, you only know that those who have been baptized have been added to the church. But what is meant by the term *church*?

Baptism—not a matter of church affiliation

Please be aware of the vicious cycle of uncertainty. To know not means to assume, to assume means to know not. We do not want to assume. We want to have clarity instead.

In Christ you are baptized into the family of God.

Therefore, let us take another passage of God's word to clarify the meaning of the term church. "For as the body is one, and hath many members, and all the members of that one body, being many, are one body: so also is Christ. For by one Spirit are we all baptized into one body, whether we be Jews or Gentiles, whether we be bond or free; and have been all made to drink into one Spirit. For the body is not one member, but many." (1 Corinthians 12:12-14) Paul clearly compares the literal physical body with the body of Christ. The main characteristic of a body is the existence of several members and their interaction. As God's children, we are one of those members of the body of Christ! These verses do not convey the message of being members of a church or local assembly, but being members of the body of Christ. We are baptized by one Spirit, the holy Spirit, into one body!

In Jesus, "there is no respect of persons with God." (Romans 2:11) Thus, no distinction exists between Jews or Gentiles. It is Jesus who "is our peace, who hath made both one, and hath broken down the middle wall of partition between us. Having abolished in his flesh the enmity, even the law of commandments contained in ordinances; for to make in himself of twain one new man, so making peace; And that he might reconcile both unto God in one body by the cross, having slain the enmity thereby." (Ephesians 2:13-15) In his body Jesus reconciled us unto God, and through baptism, we enter into this very body of Christ!

Thus, we are not baptized into a church, religious system, or the like, which religions may want to obsessively infer from passages like Acts 2:41, 46. On the contrary, we are added to the body of our precious Lord Jesus Christ by the holy Spirit. Even the sheepfold of John chapter 10 does not represent any religion, any church, or any spiritual system. It stands for the group of people who believe in Jesus Christ, accept the gift of salvation through faith, and follow the good shepherd "for they know his voice." (John 10:4) These members belong to the holy family of God and have ample reasons to rejoice in their Lord.

Baptism—the called out ones

The Greek origin of the noun church simply means a gathering of the called out ones. Nothing more, nothing less. And who are the called out ones? "Who hath delivered us from the power of darkness, and hath translated us into the kingdom of his dear Son: In whom we have redemption through his blood, even the forgiveness of sins: Who is the image of the invisible God, the firstborn of every creature: For by him were all things created, that are in heaven, and that are in earth, visible and invisible, whether they be thrones, or dominions, or principalities, or powers: all things were created by him, and for him: And he is before all things, and by him all things consist. And he is the head of the body." (Colossians 1:13-18) The called out ones are those who have experienced the spiritual regeneration, and thus have redemption through the blood of Jesus, hence forgiveness of their sins. They hear the voice of Jesus and follow him. The called out ones are those of whom Jesus says: "And I give unto them eternal life; and they shall never perish, neither shall any man pluck them out of my hand." (John 10:28) They are "passed from death unto life" (John 5:24) because they give all the glory to Jesus and proclaim with a thankful heart: "with his stripes we are healed." (Isaiah 53:5) These people who are called out trust in Jesus, who promises them the following: "For where two or three are gathered together in my name, there am I in the midst of them." (Matthew 18:20)

> The called out ones are those who hear the voice of God.

There is only one sheepfold into which we shall be added through baptism. This sheepfold is the body of Christ, the assembly of those who received Christ by grace through faith! Philip, a servant of Jesus Christ, preached the Good News about Jesus. So he did to the treasurer of the Queen of Ethiopia. The treasurer's response of having received the Gospel of Jesus Christ is recorded as follows: "Look! There's some water! Why can't I be baptized?" (Acts 8:36) The question is: What stops *you* from being baptized?

Baptism: six points to consider

You may ask yourself whether there are any steps to follow before being allowed to be baptized? It is a valid question, even though it seems to be legalistic, as if a checklist exists that needs to be fulfilled. Remember, a formal outward baptism is of no use! However, true baptism is a consequence of being born again. You want to be baptized, because you received Christ and want to participate in this act of faith. Something, or rather some*one* pushes you to do it. It is none other than the holy Spirit, who dwells in you once you received Christ in your life! This is not plain theory, but reality you will experience in your life for sure!

Here are six points to consider in the context of baptism. If you honestly can affirm each of them, it is time for you to truly ask yourself what stops you from being baptized! Let us start with the first point: *Hear the Good News, the Gospel of Jesus Christ.* Do you know who Jesus Christ is and "whosoever believeth on him shall not be ashamed"? (Romans 10:11) Do you know that there is "none other name under heaven given among men, whereby we must be saved"? (Acts 4:12)

Let us continue to the next point: *Believe in Jesus Christ!* Have you personally received Christ? Is Jesus the Savior and Lord of your life?

The third point is *to repent*! Do you want to be converted to the Lord? Being in Christ is the only way to get rid of the sinful nature and be a partaker of the divine nature.

Fourthly, *confess with your mouth the Lord Jesus Christ*! Are you proclaiming Jesus Christ and his work of salvation? Do you proclaim with one voice together with the Apostle Paul: "For I am not ashamed of the gospel of Christ: for it is the power of God unto salvation to every one that believeth; to the Jew first, and also to the Greek"? (Romans 1:16)

The subsequent point is the following: *Be baptized for the remission of sins*! Once you acknowledge Jesus as your personal Savior and Lord, you will see that you want to follow him wherever he may go and lead you to go! It is *then* that baptism is not an act of pure legalism, tradition, or outward formality, but of faith! You are buried with Jesus by baptism into death and justified, because Christ "was raised again for our justification." (Romans 4:25) As a child of God, you are now a member of the body of Christ!

The sixth and last point is to encourage you to *be faithful unto death*. Hold on to the promise of Jesus Christ. "All that the Father giveth me shall come to me; and him that cometh to me I will in no wise cast out." (John 6:37)

Jesus, the good shepherd, proclaims: "And I give unto them eternal life; and they shall never perish, neither shall any man pluck them out of my hand. My Father, which gave them me, is greater than all; and no man is able to pluck them out of my Father's hand." (John 10:28, 29) This is assurance of salvation in its most complete form. No doubt. No fear, but an unconditional *Yes* from God through Jesus Christ toward the children of God. To him be glory and honor and praise! Amen.

5: Be Of Good Cheer

"These things I have spoken unto you, that in me ye might have peace. In the world ye shall have tribulation: but be of good cheer; I have overcome the world." (John 16:33) These are indeed encouraging words of Jesus Christ. He wants you to have peace, true peace that permeates every aspect of your life. Jesus has overcome the world! Followers of Jesus Christ shall also overcome and are promised to receive God's promises. "He that overcometh shall inherit all things; and I will be his God, and he shall be my son." (Revelation 21:7) What does the term *all things* mean? Let us have a closer look at what God promises to bestow as a result of having overcome. In the book of Revelation, for instance, we find a passage about the messages to be given unto seven churches. Here, we find a lot of information about what the one who overcomes will receive.

For illustrative purposes, let us discuss some of the messages given to these churches. You will notice that in essence, each of them talks about the same outcome for the one who overcomes, and that is *eternal life.*

Promises to those who overcome

For example, the message to the angel of the church of Ephesus is described as follows: "He that hath an ear, let him hear what the Spirit saith unto the churches; To him that overcometh will I give to eat of the tree of life, which is in the midst of the paradise of God." (Revelation 2:7) Clearly, God lets us know that the one who overcomes will eat of the tree of life, which is the equivalent to living forever. "And the LORD God said, 'Behold, the man is become as one of us, to know good and evil: and now, lest he put forth his hand, and take also of the tree of life, and eat, and live for ever.' " (Genesis 3:22) The one who overcomes has eternal life!

Similarly, the message of the angel of the church in Smyrna is formulated as follows: "He that hath an ear, let him hear what the Spirit saith unto the churches; He that overcometh shall not be hurt of the second death." (Revelation 2:11) The second death is the opposite of eternal life. Thus, the one who overcomes has victory over the second death and, as a result, will live forever.

Moreover, the angel of the church in Sardis shall be given the following message: "He that overcometh, the same shall be clothed in white raiment; and I will not blot out his name out of the book of life, but I will confess his name before my Father, and before his angels." (Revelation 3:5) Read it again! This is good news! Those who overcome are not blotted out of the book of life! Everyone written in this book has access to the tree of life and victory over the second death.

Finally, the message to the angel of the church of the

Laodiceans even exceeds every conception about what follows the one who overcomes: "To him that overcometh will I grant to sit with me in my throne, even as I also overcame, and am set down with my Father in his throne." (Revelation 3:21) This verse is talking about Jesus telling those who overcome to be allowed to sit on his throne together with him! Jesus really wants to spend eternity in an intimate relationship with those who overcome.

True followers of Christ will overcome and inherit eternal life. But the question is: what do they overcome?

What shall be overcome?

The Apostle John tells us in his first epistle: "For whatsoever is born of God overcometh the world." (1 John 5:4) A born-again person overcomes the world. John describes the term *world* in a more tangible way: "Love not the world, neither the things that are in the world. If any man love the world, the love of the Father is not in him. For all that is in the world, the lust of the flesh, and the lust of the eyes, and the pride of life, is not of the Father, but is of the world. And the world passeth away, and the lust thereof: but he that doeth the will of God abideth for ever." (1 John 2:15-17) We do not need to hate the world per se, but rather, the evil things in it.

In particular, John warns us that in the last days evil manifestations will come to a head: "This know also, that in the last days perilous times shall come. For men shall be lovers of their own selves, covetous, boasters, proud, blasphemers, disobedient to parents, unthankful, unholy, without natural affection, trucebreakers, false accusers, incontinent, fierce, despisers of those that are good, traitors, heady, highminded, lovers of pleasures more than lovers of

God; Having a form of godliness, but denying the power thereof: from such turn away." (2 Timothy 3:1-5) These verses do not need any further explanation. We are in danger to have a mere form of godliness, unless we know Jesus and accepted him as Savior and Lord in our lives. Only in Christ are we protected from any type of hypocrisy.

What about those who do not overcome?

We have heard that those who overcome will have victory over the second death. The other side of the coin represents those who do not overcome. John describes those in detail: "But the fearful, and unbelieving, and the abominable, and murderers, and whoremongers, and sorcerers, and idolaters, and all liars, shall have their part in the lake which burneth with fire and brimstone: which is the second death." (Revelation 21:8) Followers of Jesus will overcome the second death.

However, the main point here is not to focus on the negatives, but to show the manifestations of sin. It is not the intention to put stress on you and to push you to change yourself restlessly, or even to stop sinning for fear of the second death and losing your name in the book of life. It is rather, a means to give you the opportunity to examine yourself!

Are you loving the things that are in the world as stated previously? Are you still happy and feeling comfortable in your sins? Do you even recognize those things of the world as sin? "Examine yourselves, whether ye be in the faith; prove your own selves. Know ye not your own selves, how that Jesus Christ is in you, except ye be reprobates?" (2 Corinthians 13:5) Ask yourself the most important question: are you in the faith?

Are you in the faith?

Are you in the faith? Your answer to this crucial question is decisive. Why? Because it literally tells you your eternal destiny! By definition, you cannot overcome those things that are in the world. Remember the words of our great Master: "I am the vine, ye are the branches: He that abideth in me, and I in him, the same bringeth forth much fruit: for without me ye can do nothing." (John 15:5) Without Jesus you cannot do anything. You are indeed helpless and in need of a Savior to deliver you from sin and its power and dominion over you.

The Good News, though, is that in Christ you get everything you need to overcome: "Who is he that overcometh the world, but he that believeth that Jesus is the Son of God?" (1 John 5:5) This is the work of Jesus Christ: to redeem you from your sinful nature and to set you free from sin itself. This leads us back to the core message of John 3:16: "whosoever believeth in him should not perish, but have everlasting life." It is not *your* effort. It is not *your* endeavor. It is not you at all. It is to believe in Jesus Christ and receive him as Savior and Lord. You are saved by grace through faith in Jesus Christ! I warmly invite you to accept God's invitation. Do not look unto you and your shortcomings but unto Jesus Christ, the Son of God, who is "the author and finisher of our faith." (Hebrews 12:2)

About The Author

Graduated in information technology, Dr. Andreas Starzacher, born in 1982 and married to his beloved wife, Barbara, whom he has four amazing children with, decided to follow Jesus Christ at the age of twelve after he had heard about the Good News, the everlasting Gospel of Jesus Christ, the Son of God. Even though Andreas was familiar with Jesus, the Gospel, and God's Word, he still longed for true freedom and peace of mind in his life. Why? Simply because he did not have it, even though he had already been a so-called born-again Christian for over two decades. This circumstance bothered him for a long time.

Finally, with the help of God guided by the holy Spirit, Andreas realized that he was merely familiar with Jesus Christ, but he did not literally *know* Jesus, in that Andreas was able to trust him completely. After having put his trust in God and his promises in Jesus Christ, Andreas embraced true freedom and peace of mind out of the hands of Jesus more and more each day. This experience is possible for everyone who dares to approach Jesus Christ through faith. A personal encounter with Jesus is not mere theory, but the utmost reality everyone can experience. Being born again in baptism through the holy Spirit, Andreas and Barbara became members of the body of Christ, that is the family of God's children.

In Christ alone you can feel secure, settled, and, most of all, loved.

"And ye shall know the truth,
and the truth shall make you free." *Jesus Christ*

www.ingramcontent.com/pod-product-compliance
Lightning Source LLC
LaVergne TN
LVHW051222200726

843510LV00011B/1449